Hiking
Green Mountain
National Forest
Southern Section

**Text, Photos, and Cartography
by Bruce Scofield**

**New England Cartographics
2000**

Cover design by Bruce Scofield

Published by New England Cartographics, Inc. All rights reserved. No part
of this book may be reproduced or transmitted in any form or by any
means, electronic or mechanical, including photocopying and recording, or
by an information storage or retrieval system, except as may be expressly
permitted by the 1976 Copyright Act or in writing from the publisher.
Requests for permission should be addressed in writing to New England
Cartographics, PO Box 9369, North Amherst, MA 01059.
Email geolopes@crocker.com   *www.necartographics.com*

Library of Congress Catalog Card Number 00-103835
Text, photography, and cartography by Bruce Scofield
Text editing and typesetting by Valerie Vaughan

Publishers Cataloging in Publication

Scofield, Bruce
    Hiking Green Mountain National Forest: southern section
/ by Bruce Scofield.
    176 p. Includes maps.
    ISBN 1-889787-06-X
    1. Hiking -- Vermont -- Guidebooks. 2. Vermont --
    Description and travel -- Guidebooks. 3. Green Mountain
    National Forest -- Guidebooks.
    796.5   00-103835

```
ATTENTION ! HIKERS:
 * Due to changes in trail conditions, the use of information
in this book is at the sole risk of the user.
 * Some trails cross through portions of private land and may not
always be open to the public. Please respect owner's rights.
```

Printed in the United States of America
10 9 8 7 6 5 4 3 2 1   06 05 04 03 02 01 00

Acknowledgments

The author would like to thank Jeff Pelton and Tony Blair of the U. S. Forest Service for their help in providing information about the subject matter in this book. Jeff Pelton was particularly helpful with the first draft of the manuscript, offering many useful suggestions and corrections. Thanks to Sylvia Plumb (from the Green Mountain Club Office) who looked over the manuscript, Matthew Cole of the U.S. Generating Company, and Kevin O'Toole who shared his knowledge of the trails near Dorset. I'd like to thank Valerie Vaughan who edited the manuscript and also accompanied me on some of my many exploratory treks to southern Vermont.

About the Author

Bruce Scofield is the author of several hiking guides, including *50 Hikes in New Jersey, High Peaks of the Northeast, Hiking the Pioneer Valley*, and *Fodor's Short Escapes Near Boston*. Scofield earns his living primarily from a private astrological consulting practice. He is also the author of several books on astrology, including two on the astrology of ancient Mesoamerica (Maya, Toltec, Aztec). He lives in Amherst, Massachusetts.

Table of Contents

Chapter 5: Hiking the Mountains   87

Chapter 6: Hiking to the Ponds   123

Chapter 7: Day-Hiking and Backpacking Trips   153

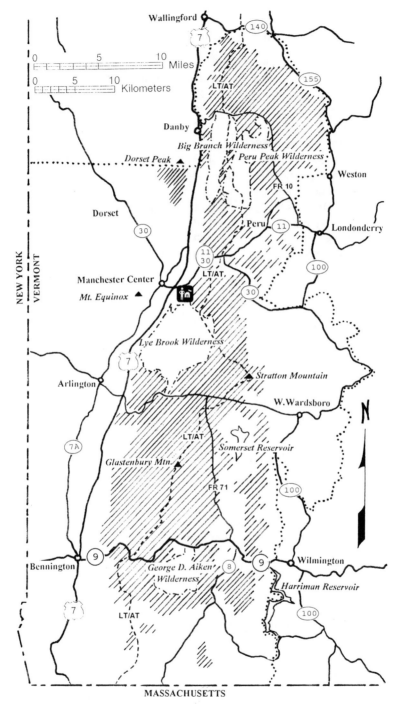

Map showing the approximate boundaries (dotted line) of the southern section of the Green Mountain National Forest. The actual public land is shown by the diagonal lines.

6

Introduction

The Green Mountain National Forest preserves 370,000 acres of forest in the state of Vermont. The forest is divided into two sections, north and south, with a substantial gap of private land separating them. This hiking guide covers only the southern section, an area of 230,373 acres (as of 1999), extending from the Massachusetts border to Vermont Route 140. There is a forthcoming guide to the northern section which is now in preparation.

The southern section of the Green Mountain National Forest is a large and unique parcel of public land that contains four wilderness areas, mostly without trails, and includes many large roadless areas. Its location near centers of high population makes it a valuable resource for those who seek a direct contact with nature. Although the Forest does not have any skyscraping alpine summits or mile-high cliffs and canyons, it has much to offer hikers, backpackers and seekers of a wilderness experience. Visitors to the Forest who climb to one of the high mountain lookouts will discover a vast, high plateau of ponds, meadows, brooks and bogs. Visitors may also have surprising encounters with wildlife in this wild forest and they will find that it offers great camping opportunities.

Visitors shouldn't let the rounded shapes of the mountains lead them into thinking the area poses no challenges. The vastness of this high Eastern forest should be taken seriously. If you are the kind of person who is sensitive to nature's more subtle manifestations, one who sees beauty in wild and remote mountain meadows, wilderness ponds alive with both the tiny sundew and the stately moose, and wooded summits with lookouts that reveal miles of uninterrupted woodland, then you will enjoy this National Forest. There are very few places left in the Northeast where one can completely escape the mechanized and stressful world of humanity. The Green Mountain National Forest is one of those places.

The Green Mountain National Forest has much to offer hikers and backpackers. It has an extensive trail network, the spine of which is the Long Trail (**LT**) and the Appalachian Trail (**AT**), which share a common route. The presence of the Green Mountain Club's (GMC) Long Trail, and its side trail network, has long been a focus of activity for hikers. The mere presence of the Long Trail has also played an important role in protecting many highly scenic areas from logging or development for intensive, high-impact recreation. The Long Trail and its side trails are not the only areas of the National Forest that offer opportunities to hikers, however. Many other areas exist which are covered in this guide.

Hikers visiting the southern section of the Green Mountain National Forest will soon realize that this National Forest differs significantly from the White Mountain National Forest in neighboring New Hampshire. The White Mountains have a more extensive trail network that is maintained by powerful and well-established hiking organizations. In the southern section of the Green Mountain National Forest, hikers are only one of several large user groups. Snowmobiles have a very strong presence in the Forest, hunting has a long history, dispersed car-camping is still allowed, and there is a growing use (both legal and illegal) of SUVs and ATVs.

Hikers who choose to explore areas of the Green Mountain National Forest other than those areas traversed by the Long Trail/Appalachian Trail (LT/AT) may find evidence of other, more aggressive use of natural lands. The Green Mountain National Forest is a big area that is shared by many different kinds of users. The Forest Service has long struggled with the problems that arise from the conflicting interests of logging operations, ski resort development, motorized vs. non-motorized uses, and the protection of habitats and species. At the present time, the Forest Service seems to be maintaining a delicate balance between these user groups.

We live in an age of user conflicts. Corporations constantly offer products that allow people to aggressively dominate nature, and their enticing advertisements suggest that these products will somehow enhance the status of the consumer. After shelling out a considerable sum for such products, consumers are likely to assume that this gives them the right to use these products freely on public land. From the hiker's point of view, there is concern today for the preservation of the trails and the protection of the trail environment itself. It's certainly one of the things that makes hiking the activity I've come to love. I would like to see the hiking trail system in the Forest expanded, in particular toward more loop hikes. In order for trail quality to be maintained and expansion to be possible, it's important that hikers maintain good relations with the Forest Service.

Hikers ask for very little in the way of conveniences; we build our own trails, and most of us keep the forest clean. Unlike the snowmobilers or hunters, hikers are not required to have a permit or register with the Forest Service in any way. As a result, most hikers are not associated with an organized user group. Because many hikers are not hiking club members, our numbers are not always known. This means that the hiking lobby in the Green Mountain National Forest is essentially the Green Mountain Club. Therefore, I urge all who hike in the Forest to consider joining the Green Mountain Club, the strongest lobby for our relatively benign use of the Forest. And I also urge hikers to uphold the guidelines and high ideals set by the GMC in regard to the use of trails and camping areas.

How to Use This Book

This guide is organized in a somewhat different manner than many other hiking guides. Instead of simply listing a series of hike descriptions by number, I've chosen to approach the subject by describing three primary natural features of interest to hikers -- the wilderness areas, the mountains, and the ponds. First-hand anecdotal information about these features will convey to the reader a better sense of what to expect in the areas described, and will hopefully make for more interesting reading. Following these three main features are descriptions of several challenging circular day-hikes or backpacks that involve the use of only one car. In addition to data related purely to hiking, readers will find information that can make a visit to the area more meaningful, such as the geology and history of the region, the history of the Forest Service in southern Vermont, the towns that surround the Forest, and a description of the many other outdoor activities that take place within the area. Knowing more about where you are hiking makes for a more interesting trip.

Preparation for Hiking

Hiking is not really a sport, it is more of a multifaceted activity that can include good exercise, companionship, the aesthetic appreciation of nature, photography, and the study of rocks, plants and animals. While there may be extremes on the curve of hikers that might use this book (from trail runners to nature walkers), most are somewhere in between. For whatever reasons one chooses to hike, it is wise to prepare for some of the things that may happen on the trail by having the right attitude and bringing along the right equipment. Here are some guidelines which hikers should follow in order to protect themselves, others and the natural environment.

Be sure that you are in the right physical condition for the amount of hiking you choose to do. If you are not sure of what you are capable of, take a few shorter hikes to test yourself. Pace yourself and work up gradually to the longer hikes listed in Chapter 7; don't plunge into a situation that may be beyond your capabilities. Backpackers especially should take this advice. The extra weight of backpacking equipment must be considered when making a choice about where to hike.

Hikers should sign in at all trail registers. Be sure to write where you are from, your trip itinerary, and then sign out again on your return. Also, tell people you know exactly where you are planning to hike and when you plan to return. Search-and-rescue is expensive.

First on the list of equipment for hiking is footwear. The wrong shoes can ruin a hike. Many serious hikers prefer the traditional leather hiking boot with rugged soles. Today's lightweight hiking boots, some with ankle collars and air cushioned soles, are extremely comfortable and very rugged. These boots can take a dunking and they have a tread that grips rocks quite well. In warmer weather, some hikers prefer wearing good quality running shoes. In cold and wet weather, rubber bottomed boots with leather uppers and felt liners are appropriate. Under icy conditions, which may last into spring on the northern and more shaded slopes of the mountains, some type of ice cramp-on is essential. Small, four-toothed in-step cramp-ons are inexpensive and can make a slippery descent much safer. With deep snows, snowshoes are appropriate, particularly those designed with bindings on an axle that make climbing easy. Some trails described in this book may be tried on cross-country skis under the right conditions. In the higher elevations of the Green Mountains, snow may linger well into the month of May. Be prepared for this possibility by carrying some kind of cramp-on or snow cleat.

Socks are important too. Once they get wet, cotton socks will stay wet and can be very uncomfortable in cold weather. Wool and synthetic fabrics are warm even when wet and they dry faster. An extra pair of socks should always be carried on overnight trips or when rain is a possibility.

Day-hikers should carry a daypack with a few essentials in it. The daypack itself need not be excessively large, but it should be comfortable and capable of carrying some extra clothing, particularly in winter. For very short hikes in summer, a fanny-pack may be sufficient. In the pack you should always carry a first aid kit, a water bottle or canteen (carry water from home or purify with a filter or iodine), a pocket knife, a map and compass, small flashlight, length of cord or string (good for tying things onto your pack), rain gear of some sort, tissues or toilet paper, and some food. Hikers might also carry certain items that they require personally such as sunscreen, glasses, tampons, or medications. Bring along some moleskin for blisters; it is available in the foot section of drugstores.

Proper clothing for each season is a must. A layering system is recommended in which several items are worn or taken off as needed. Synthetic fabrics, such as poly-pro and fleece, are far better in wet and cold weather than cotton and are highly recommended for the layer closest to your skin. Wool is also a good insulator that works even when wet. During the late spring, summer, and early fall be sure to bring along some insect repellent. Lyme disease, transmitted by ticks, is not common in this area, but every hiker should know something about it and how to prevent it.

You might find it convenient to keep the basic items like the knife, compass, flashlight, etc., in a ditty bag which fits in your pack and can be taken out easily if a different pack is worn. Wide-mouth water bottles are preferable to canteens. They come in many sizes and are unbreakable and leakproof.

It rains often in the Green Mountains. The recommended rain gear is a rainsuit, consisting of a hooded top and pants. You can also use a parka shell for rain, wind, and as an extra layer in cold conditions. A poncho is another possibility and can also double as a makeshift shelter (using the length of cord mentioned above), although a rainsuit is much better protection in wind-driven rains. Plastic ponchos, parka shells, or rainpants may be waterproof, but they are not comfortable for extensive hiking as they don't allow for air circulation. They will keep moisture out, but they keep it in as well. Some of the newer fabrics like Gore*tex tend to breathe better and are more comfortable for active hiking in the rain, though you will pay steeply for this luxury item.

Backpackers will, of course, need to carry more than day-hikers. Those seeking an overnight experience will need to bring along a sleeping bag. Since much of the Green Mountain National Forest is at an elevation of over 2,000 feet, backpackers should be prepared for colder temperatures than may be predicted by local radio or television stations. Temperatures at night can be downright cool even at the height of summer. At high elevations, freezing temperatures can occur as early as September and as late as May. It's important to know what your sleeping bag is capable of. In addition to a sleeping bag, backpackers should carry some kind of ground insulation. The lightest and most economical, though not the most comfortable, is a simple closed-cell foam pad. More expensive ground pads, combinations of closed-cell and air mattress, are available and can make your night sleeping out more enjoyable.

Backpackers may be able to find floor space for sleeping in one of the many shelters maintained by the Green Mountain Club. By camping out of season or avoiding the weekends, the chances are improved of having plenty of room at a shelter, and even having it to yourself. At the high-use areas, described elsewhere in this guide, fees may be charged by GMC caretakers on duty. Backpackers hiking to such areas should not count on shelter space, particularly during weekends. A tent, or at least a tarp, should be carried in case of crowding. Shelter etiquette, which may be enforced by a GMC caretaker if necessary, means sharing a shelter with those who arrive after you do -- until all the reasonable floor space is taken. Late-comers to shelters who find them full should camp with their tents nearby and not force themselves into an already crowded space.

A final word on trails themselves is appropriate here. Trails should not be taken for granted. Somebody, or some group, usually keeps them in good shape and cleans them up on a regular basis. The Long Trail/Appalachian Trail and their side trails are maintained by volunteers. The Forest Service also maintains trails. Please respect the work others have done for your benefit by carrying out anything you bring into the forest. Many trails are not maintained for hikers. Some multi-use trails may not provide a solid or dry surface, may be rutted by motorized recreational vehicles, and may be littered in places. Please help to keep all trails clean. If you are interested in doing any trail maintenance, a volunteer activity that is quite rewarding, contact the GMC or the Forest Service (for address, telephone and other contact information, see page 28 or 172).

Where to Get Maps

Hikers should know how to read a topographic map and use a compass. The maps in this guide should provide hikers with enough information for most of the mountains and ponds, but the maps of the wilderness areas in this book are not detailed enough for practical use. Hikers venturing into any of the wilderness areas should prepare themselves by studying a topographical map ahead of time, and then bring this map (and a compass) with them on the hike. The lack of trails in the wilderness areas of the National Forest provides opportunities for land navigation, but exploration of these remote areas is definitely not for the inexperienced.

Maps of the Green Mountain National Forest may be obtained in person or by mail from the Manchester Ranger District office on Routes 11 & 30, about one mile east of the Route 7 overpass. The most useful maps for hikers are the USGS topographic maps, provisional editions, which clearly indicate the public lands managed by the Forest Service. These maps show all the Forest roads, snowmobile routes, and trails. Most, though not all, are metric, and indicate elevations and distances in meters and kilometers. These maps sold for $4.00 per quad in 1999. The Forest Service also has free maps of the wilderness areas called "The Wilderness Times." These maps have contours and they highlight some of the features of each area, but they are not recommended for wilderness land navigation.

The Green Mountain Club publishes a set of maps called "End To End" which show the route of the Long Trail on a four-color topographic map. While these maps are very well made, they do not show the many Forest Roads and snowmobile trails that hikers need to know about if they are exploring portions of the National Forest that are off the Long Trail. Similar, though less detailed, maps are contained in the invaluable *Long Trail Guide*, also published by the Green Mountain Club.

Chapter 1

The Green Mountain National Forest

The Green Mountain National Forest covers a substantial portion of southern Vermont. While it contains some very large roadless areas, not all of it is wilderness. It is bounded on the east and west by major roads and is crossed by several others. Houses, both first and second homes, and commercial establishments line these roads. Throughout the year, tourists in automobiles drive along these paved edges of roadless areas, but few enter on foot. Four ski areas figure prominently within the overall boundaries of the Green Mountain National Forest, some of them utilizing Forest Service land through lease arrangements. Two huge reservoirs lie in its midst and a group of wind generators whirl atop a Searsburg peak, all being sources of electric power.

The condition of the forest was different in pre-Colonial times than it is today. First, there was a lot more forest. The only major breaks were where ponds or marshes had flooded out the trees, or where fires had broken out. These openings were small, 99% less than a quarter acre. Five hundred years ago, the predominant species of the region were sugar maple, beech, and red spruce, these being what are called late-successional species. Early successional species such as paper birch, red maple, and balsam fir, which are the species that dominate the forest today, were found in fewer numbers. On the lower hillsides were huge pines, perhaps as high as 200 feet and five to six feet in diameter. In higher elevations, fir and spruce toughed out the difficult growing conditions, as they do today.

With the European colonists came the cutting of trees. At first the wood was used for building homes, furniture, and for heating. The larger, perfectly straight monster pines were cut and shipped via special ships to be used for masts for the British Navy. The hunger for lumber was continuous. The American Revolution may have stopped the flow of wood out of Vermont and back to England, but it also stimulated the domestic need for quality wood for gunstocks and charcoal to feed the kilns that made iron -- all to fuel the war effort.

Wood was cut in Vermont and floated down tributary rivers to the Connecticut River in great log drives. Lake Champlain was also used to transport logs north to markets in Canada. By the mid-19th century, Burlington, Vermont, ranked third in the country as a wholesale lumber market. The barge canal to Albany was yet another route that the timber felled in Vermont followed on its way to market.

Virgin red spruce made up a large portion of the lumber shipped out of Vermont during the 19th century. This light weight, but very strong wood was used for many products, including clapboards, boxes, boats, and musical instruments. By 1900, Vermont had become the fourth largest producer of this wood in the United States. It's been said that nowhere in North America were more forests cut down and consequently, more soils eroded, than in Vermont's Green Mountains. The forest we see here today is a far cry from the original forest. It takes something like 350 years before a forest can recover fully from such a severe cutting as took place here in the Green Mountains.

The Dawning of the Environmental Movement

It was George Perkins Marsh of Woodstock, Vermont, who first spoke out against the insanity of the forest industry. Marsh was a successful lawyer and a founder of the Smithsonian Institution. He had also served in Congress. His 1864 publication *Man in Nature* became an international best-seller and was instrumental in fueling the conservation movement of the late 19th century. In it he attacked the wasteful ways of the logging industry, but he also offered solutions.

As early as 1847 Marsh was challenging the people of Vermont with his observations concerning the waste and devastation left behind by the logging business. By that time most of Vermont's forests were privately owned and the millions of sheep grazing on the land were preventing the forest from growing back. Then, as now, the average person was so preoccupied with the necessities of personal survival and the raising of a family that the cultural change required to remedy the situation was just not possible. Habits tend to be altered only when things get really, really bad. But things did get bad for the forests. By 1900, only 20% of Vermont was covered by forest; 80% was cleared land.

There were others in Vermont who challenged this undeclared war on nature. Joseph Battell had visited Europe early in his life and was deeply affected by the respect given to forests there. He later pressured the Vermont government to stop the abuse of the forests by industrial interests. Battell was also an animal lover and hotel keeper. He ran the Bread Loaf Inn on land that is now part of the northern section of the Green Mountain National Forest, and was known to have turned guests away for arriving by automobile instead of by horse.

14

In 1891, Battell made a particularly passionate plea before the Vermont State Legislature to save the mountains. He painted a gloomy picture of forest devastation, blaming timber butchers, lumber merchants, and fire bugs who were spoiling the natural landscape of Vermont. His efforts, along with those of others, became known as "the forestry movement" by 1900. But it took some disastrous forest fires in 1903 to change public opinion. The first state forester was appointed in 1908, and by 1912 the State of Vermont finally began to appropriate some money for state forests.

An advocate for sane forestry around this same period was Marshall J. Hapgood, for whom the Green Mountain National Forest's Hapgood Pond is named. He was a forest owner who ran his lumber business in a manner that seems logical to us today, but was unusual at the time. After cutting his trees, he replanted. Not able to convince his neighbors of the wisdom of his methods, he went to the federal government, appealing to the administration of Theodore Roosevelt. He proposed to them another radical idea, that the government buy back the Vermont forest and manage it according to his methods. He even offered some of his own property as an incentive to get the process going.

It took some time for Hapgood's idea to catch on, and it also took the help of Vermont senator Redfield Proctor and Gifford Pinchot of Connecticut. At that time Pinchot was the head of a division of the Interior Department which managed some 100 million acres of government land called the Forest Reserves. In 1905, a law sponsored by Proctor and others was signed by Theodore Roosevelt, creating the Department of Agriculture, a new government agency which was to have authority over the lands of these Forest Reserves. Pinchot, later known as "the father of American forestry," was placed at the head of this new department, and this is how the U.S. Forest Service was born.

Pinchot recognized that preservation of land in one place did not necessarily protect it from damages done to unprotected places in the general region. For example, clear-cutting a forest can lower the water absorbing capacity of the soil and is one cause of the flooding of lands downstream. This issue was addressed by Senator John Weeks of Massachusetts in 1911 when he proposed what became known as the Weeks Act. This new law allowed for cooperative arrangements between the states and the federal government for land acquisition to protect watersheds and timber. The Weeks Act led to the establishment of National Forests in the West and in New Hampshire.

15

By 1909 the Vermont state government had created the position of State Forester and with it, the possibility of creating state forests. Still, nothing much happened right away. In 1925, the State proposed to the federal government the idea of a national forest in Vermont. Once again, it took some serious trouble to initiate change. The flood of 1927, which cost the state 35 million dollars, made the population desperate enough to support the idea. On December 12, 1928, the authorization for a National Forest in Vermont finally came through from the federal government. Hapgood, who died in 1927, didn't live to see some of his land become part of the first tract of 1,842 acres acquired for the new national forest.

The official creation of the Vermont National Forest came on April 25, 1932, in the middle of the Depression, but the timing turned out to be right in many ways. Vermonters living in poverty could sell their land for some cash, while the government could get on with its assignment of building up a sizable forest. Some corporations donated land, including the International Paper Company, Emporium Forestry Company, and Bellows Falls Ice Company. Large private land owners, like Silas Griffith and Peggy Beckwith donated and sold land also. Each holding was but one part of a jig-saw puzzle in a designated region that was outlined at the creation of the forest. By 1975, some 6,000 individual pieces had been acquired. This was totally unlike the National Forests of the West where land came in huge chunks with squared-off borders.

The White Mountain National Forest, which began back in 1912, was where the first headquarters of the new Vermont National Forest were located. As land acquisition increased, and a proposed purchase of 205,000 acres in north central Vermont became immanent, the need to be closer to the forest led to a move to Vermont. On November 11, 1935, seven employees moved files, record books, and themselves by truck to Rutland, Vermont. In 1937 those new 205,000 acres were approved by the federal government and signed into law by Franklin Roosevelt. These became the core of the Middlebury and Rochester Ranger Districts of today, the northern section of the Green Mountain National Forest.

The Civilian Conservation Corps

President Franklin D. Roosevelt launched the Civilian Conservation Corps in 1933, which came to be known as the C.C.C. Like the Works Progress Administration (W.P.A.), the C.C.C. was basically an employment vehicle for many people who were affected by the Depression. Forests throughout the country were "improved" with work done by this army of out-of-work men.

Camps were established to house the corps who cleared trails, built roads and ponds, stocked fish, and stabilized embankments. At first these camps were merely clusters of tents; eventually they consisted of barracks and common buildings. Many of these camps later became Boy Scout camps or lodges of one sort or another. The Bascom Lodge on the summit of Mt. Greylock in northwestern Massachusetts was a C.C.C. project, as was the White Rocks picnic area. The corps worked on the ski trails at Bromley and Breadloaf and they built today's Hapgood Pond, a major enlargement of the earlier mill pond. Other works of the C.C.C. are the road from Danby to Weston (Forest Road 10), the Greendale Recreation Area, the picnic area at Texas Falls, and some improvements along the Long Trail.

With close to 700 C.C.C workers swarming over the forest and building ponds, picnic areas, and recreational paths, Vermonters became concerned that the forest was becoming more and more like a national park. In 1937 a law was passed by the State legislature making it more difficult for forest land to be transferred to the federal government. Previously, any land sale had to be approved by the State Board on National Forests and the owner had to be willing to sell. This new state law required any transfer of land to also be approved by the local town governments. This stipulation, which gives much power to the local communities, is apparently unique in the United States.

Following the C.C.C., other government programs brought workers to Vermont's forests. The Job Corps of the 1960s, a part of Lyndon Johnson's Great Society program, did some road and trail improvements. During the 1970s the Youth Conservation Corps (Y.C.C.) brought inner city youth to the region during the summer to work on clearing and other maintenance projects. The Young Adult Conservation Corps (Y.A.C.C.) did heavier work during the same period. Both the Y.C.C. and the Y.A.C.C. shut down in 1980. Today you will still find some volunteers working around Green Mountain National Forest. The Vermont Youth Conservation Corps have helped to run the Hapgood Pond Recreation Area.

Vermont's forests have been growing so that the state is now 80% forested, a complete reversal of the conditions just eighty years ago. Of course, most of this is second growth, not a climax forest which will take another 200 or 300 years to mature. But progress has been made. Under the stewardship of the U.S. Department of Agriculture, i.e. the Forest Service, the Green Mountain National Forest is the legacy of years of struggle by forward-thinking individuals like Marsh, Battell, Hapgood, and Pinchot. Carrying on this tradition, the present day managers of this great resource work at balancing three important factors: intelligent logging, preservation of wildlife habitat, and recreational opportunities.

The boundaries of the southern section of the Green Mountain National Forest extend from the New York border east to roughly Route 100. An upper "head" is bounded by Routes 7, 140, and 155. This is the area within which Forest land may be acquired, though as of 1999, the percentage of public land within these boundaries is still only about 50%. With the exception of the central contiguous parcels through which the Long Trail passes, large areas are privately held. Scattered throughout the area are small towns, villages, private residences, and camps that are surrounded by National Forest. Hikers visiting the area should be aware of this, and they should know something about the people and the industries that have been here for centuries. Such information will be presented in the next chapter.

Logging in the Forest

The Green Mountain National Forest is organized into three ranger districts: Manchester, Middlebury, and Rochester, each with its own supervisor. Actual lumbering is done by private loggers who bid for the right to cut, but their work is overseen by the professional foresters. There are many checks and balances that figure into any logging operation. Environmental impact studies are performed and a review of cultural resources evaluates potential damage to historic sites. There's also a 45-day waiting period before work can actually commence.

In earlier times, timber sales produced a clear profit. Today, however, the checks and balances and the greater number of employees have made timber sales more financially complex. Most of the profits from sales go back to the federal Department of Agriculture, but 25% of gross receipts, plus land use fees, goes back to the local towns, all 38 of them.

Here's how it works. The federal government does not pay taxes on the land that it owns within the town boundaries, but it does pay the figure mentioned above, plus money generated from recreational uses of the land. All the towns share in the profits, whether or not their town land was harvested. This allows the National Forest to manage the area according to their models and it precludes any town from demanding to have its trees cut to produce more money for them. As would be expected, the annual revenue to towns changes from year to year, depending on how much forest was being logged. The towns like the arrangement because the land remains in their town in usually the same condition, but money is collected from it.

There have been some serious objections to logging. In early 1993 the Forest Service announced plans to log the section of the National Forest that is bounded by Route 9 on the north, the Harriman Reservoir on the east, Route 100 on the south, and Route 8 on the west. This area is known as the Lamb Brook area, named for one of the streams that drains it. It's a fairly remote area, penetrated by an old stagecoach road that was abandoned around 1820, a snowmobile trail, and Forest Road 266. This latter road was said to have been illegally constructed in 1989. According to the Forest Watch, an environmental organization, the proposed logging project would not only destroy parts of this isolated wilderness, it would have been conducted at a financial loss of about $110,000. In 1994 a coalition of environmental activists filed a lawsuit to stop the project, which at the time of this writing, has not been settled. Forest Watch has also suggested that, rather than logging this area, which encompasses just over 5,000 acres, it should instead be made a wilderness area. If you want information on Forest Watch, you can contact them at 10 Langdon Street, Montpelier, VT 05602, 802-223-3216, or the website *www.forestwatch.org.*

Western vista from the LT/AT north of Glastenbury Mountain

Recreation in the Forest

Over the past few decades, recreational use of the Green Mountain National Forest has increased. The forest has become a playground for all kinds of users, including hunters, snowmobilers, bicyclists, car campers, and, of course, hikers and backpackers. Regarding the use of the forest, the Forest Service's philosophical shift from logging to recreation began in the 1960s and appears to have settled into a position that steers away from direct competition with private recreational interests. For example, the campgrounds in the National Forest don't offer the modern amenities that most of the private campgrounds do. However, trail systems and parking areas, which allow access to different parts of the forest, are provided and maintained by the federal agency. The following sections explain how Green Mountain National Forest handles the varied recreational interests of the general public.

Hiking

The Forest offers excellent opportunities for hiking; hence this book. There are trails for every kind of hiker, or walker, from narrow footpaths up steep inclines to wide woods roads that lead to scenic ponds. The Green Mountain Club (GMC), which cooperates with the Forest, is the organization that has done more for hiking in the region than any other. A history of this important group will be found in Chapter 3.

The white-blazed Long Trail and Appalachian Trail form the spine of the hiking trail network of the Green Mountain National Forest.

In this guidebook the trail is abbreviated **LT/AT** *to emphasize the precedence of the Long Trail, even though it is abbreviated elsewhere as AT/LT.*

The LT/AT is routed so that it passes near many scenic areas, and a traveler following its path will be afforded a kind of grand tour of the Forest. Side trails off the LT/AT are normally marked in blue. In a few places, long loop hikes are possible which lead hikers to other interesting places, and these are discussed in Chapter 7. Trailheads for hikers are found where the LT/AT crosses major roads, and even some minor forest roads. Most of the parking areas for these trailheads offer a directory with relevant information posted, and some even have sanitary facilities. Although the Green Mountain Club works with the Forest Service, it does not build trailhead parking areas or maintain the directories.

Mountain Biking

Mountain bikes and any motorized vehicles are not allowed on the LT/AT or in the wilderness areas. While opportunities for mountain biking exist in Green Mountain National Forest, I haven't observed much use. This may be due to the fact that the kinds of trails that many mountain bikers prefer, such as narrow, muddy ones with extreme descents, are only open to hikers. What's left for bikers are miles and miles of gravel and dirt roads routed through dense forest, occasionally passing a meadow, and even more rarely, a long-distance view. Private ski areas, like Mt. Snow, have more to offer those who seek awesome, extreme challenges. There, a biker can take his bike on a chair lift to the summit and then barrel down the slopes to the base lodge.

Personally, I support this use of the ski slopes by mountain bikers and would not like to see them on hiking trails. My reasons for this position are threefold. Bikes damage trails, especially wet areas, far more so than boots. Second, the intrusion into nature of an elaborate mechanical gadget takes away from the experience of nature by hikers. Third, mountain bikers generally do not build the trails or maintain them. I do support the building and maintenance of separate mountain bike trails by mountain biking clubs, under the supervision of the Forest Service, as long as they don't conflict with hiking trails. This kind of arrangement has already been made by snowmobile groups as we will see below.

Snowmobiles

During winter, snowmobiles have a strong presence in Green Mountain National Forest, and each one is capable of emitting up to 100 times the carbon monoxide and 300 times the hydrocarbons of a single car. Southern Vermont is a major center for this sport. The largest snowmobile club in the country, the 5,000 member Woodford Snowbusters, is based here. Weekend usage by club members is very high and several snowmobile tour companies exist that offer excursions (for about $50 per hour) into the heart of the Green Mountain National Forest. "Snowmobile Central" is probably the Woodford Mall, located high on Route 9 between Wilmington and Bennington. A drive along this section of Route 9 on a nice winter weekend will reveal the extent to which this Forest user group has established itself.

Snowmobile operators have their own umbrella organization, the Vermont Association of Snow Travelers, Inc. (VAST), which in turn has many member clubs. The name is certainly apt because VAST, with 32,000 members, is huge. Compare this with the Green Mountain Club which has 8,000 members.

VAST has developed a statewide system of trail corridors which pass through the Forest using old logging roads and unplowed dirt roads, but not hiking trails. They cooperate extensively with the Forest Service which provides them with large trailhead parking areas. VAST negotiates with the many private landowners within the National Forest to obtain permission for their members to pass over their properties.

The Forest Service encourages snowmobilers to become members of VAST. It is only through a strong club like VAST that user conflicts can be resolved and control over restricted areas can be maintained. (Note that the Forest service has no jurisdiction over snowmobile routes that traverse private land without the landowners' permission, this being a matter for local law enforcement authorities.) Membership in a group encourages a collective set of rules and regulations, and punishes reckless individual behaviors. With many people operating such a powerful recreational device as a snowmobile, it's necessary to have some controls in place.

The use of snowmobiles in the Forest was given a boost when the State of Vermont gave a grant to the National Forest to develop snowmobile trails. Snowmobile routes through the forest were soon established and were called corridors. Corridor 7, known as C7 (and referred to locally as I-91), is a major north-south route that intersects hiking trails in some places. There are many, many snowmobile routes north and south of the Woodford area, and one of them actually climbs Glastenbury Mountain.

Just south of Woodford, Forest Road 73 is now open during winter months only (when snow depth is over 6 inches) for All Terrain Vehicle (ATV) use. This is said to be a 12-mile test trail system. Maps of these routes are available from businesses that cater to motorized snow recreationalists. The Forest Service has also published a winter use map that shows the major snowmobile routes, though this map is out-of-date and may not be republished. Snowmobiles, or any kind of mechanized transportation, are not allowed in any of the wilderness areas.

Cross Country Skiing and Snowshoeing

Throughout the Green Mountain National Forest, the many miles of foot trails, woods roads and logging roads are open to ski touring and snowshoeing. Cross-country skiers should not expect any amenities, other than some trailhead parking areas provided by the Forest Service, which are primarily parking areas for all the trucks, SUVs, and trailers that transport snowmobiles. Those who delight in the peaceful atmosphere of backcountry ski touring may find the wilderness areas in the Forest ideal, since they are off-limits to vehicles. Outside of wilderness areas, skiers should keep very alert for snowmobile traffic.

Cross country skiers interested in skiing in the Green Mountain National Forest should know about the Catamount Trail Association. This volunteer, non-profit organization is very much like a hiking club. It is concerned with the creation and maintenance of a statewide ski corridor that, like the Long Trail, will eventually follow the Green Mountain range from the Massachusetts border all the way to Canada. About 60% of this route is presently open and some inn-to-inn skiing opportunities are possible. The Harriman Trail, along the west shore of the Harriman Reservoir, is a part of this trail. For more information, you can contact the Catamount Trail Association at PO Box 897, Burlington, VT 05402, phone 802- 864-5794.

There are several nordic/cross-country ski areas within the boundaries of Green Mountain National Forest. Most of these charge about $10 to $15 for the use of their groomed trails, lodge, warming huts, and other amenities. Prospect Mountain Ski Touring Center is located high on Route 9 in the middle of (but not overlapping) snowmobile territory. This center has a small alpine area, which has been closed for some years now, and an extensive trail system of 35 kilometers. One trail, the Mountain Trail, runs very close to the George D. Aiken Wilderness area which Prospect Mountain is adjacent to.

There are three cross country centers near the Mount Snow/Haystack downhill ski areas. The White House of Wilmington, a country inn located on Route 9, has in the past offered 37 km of trail, as well as tubing down the wide and steep front lawn of the Inn. Recent winters have been difficult for cross-country skiing, so snowshoeing on these trails is now being promoted. The extensive Hermitage Cross Country Ski Area is tucked into the eastern face of the Haystack-Mount Snow ridge. They offer 50 km of trails on varied terrain. Timber Creek is opposite Mount Snow, at a higher elevation which helps to ensure enough snow.

Stratton Mountain Winter Sports Area, which is mostly the Stratton Mountain downhill area plus an abundance of condos and other slope-side housing, offers two cross country possibilities. One is on a golf course, the other in the woods. In the vicinity of Peru and Weston are several skiing areas, including Wild Wings and the Viking Nordic Center. Addresses and telephone numbers for these areas are given below.

Cross Country Ski Areas

The Hermitage Cross Country Ski Area
> Coldbrook Road, Wilmington VT 05363
> 802-464-3511
> *www.hermitageinn.com*
> hermitag @ sover.net

Prospect Mountain
> Route 9, Woodford VT 05201
> 802-442-2575
> FAX: 802-423-5017   E-mail: xcski @ sover.net

Timber Creek Cross Country Ski Area
> West Dover VT 05351
> 802-464-0999

Viking Nordic Center
> RR 1, Box 70, Little Pond Road [off Route 11],
> Londonderry VT 05148   802-824-3933

The White House Cross Country Ski Touring Center
> Route 9, Wilmington VT 05363
> 802-464-2136   800-541-2135

Wild Wings Ski Touring Center
> Peru VT 05152
> 802-824-6793
> *www.floodbrookkl2.vt.us/ww/wildwings.html*

Downhill Skiing

Downhill or alpine skiing has been and continues to be a major force in the Green Mountain National Forest. Four large areas presently exist within the boundaries of the Forest that serve as four-season tourist centers -- Mount Snow, Haystack, Stratton Mountain, and Bromley. Two of these lease Forest Service land; the other two border on it. This can affect hikers, as in the case of limited access to the summit (Mount Snow) or to other parts of the mountain (Haystack Mountain). Another effect is that hikers can no longer experience a natural setting on the summits of these four mountains. The histories of these areas are told in detail in Chapter 2.

Hunting and Fishing

Hikers should be aware of the fact that hunting is permitted throughout Green Mountain National Forest. Although most serious hunting occurs during the fall and early winter months, there is some kind of hunting permitted at all times of the year. Unlike some other nearby states, hunting is also allowed on Sundays. Here's a rough guide to some of the various hunting seasons in 1998. Please note that these dates may vary. You can obtain a current hunting schedule from the appropriate ranger district headquarters.

Bobcat	mid January through mid February
Muskrat	mid March through mid April
Turkey	May, and October through November
Black Bear	September through mid November
Crow	mid March through April, and mid Aug. through Oct.
Deer (includes guns and bow & arrow)	October through mid December
Coyote, Bobwhite Quail, Chukar Partridge	no closed season.

Hunting and fishing regulations are in accordance with the Vermont Digest of Fish and Wildlife Laws. This is a 100+ page annual publication that is available free from Vermont Fish and Wildlife in Waterbury VT. You can find it at hunting and fishing stores, and it can sometimes be picked up at Chamber of Commerce offices. Licenses may be obtained from Town Clerk offices and some stores.

There are many rules and regulations that apply to hunting and fishing. For example, hunters should keep at least 500 feet from any trail or road, and hunters are asked to avoid shooting across trails or roads. Hunting is not permitted within 500 feet of camping areas, trail shelters, picnic sites, or buildings. All of the Green Mountain National Forest is open to hunters, including the wilderness areas. To report any fishing or hunting violation, the toll-free number to call is 1-800-75ALERT.

Car-Camping

Car-camping is what people do when they drive into a developed camp site and either sleep in their car or in a tent set up next to it. At the typical car-camp site, there will be a fireplace of some sort and a picnic table. Some kind of toilet facilities, a water pump, and maybe even showers and a camp store may also be within a short walk. I've car-camped many times (in a VW microbus) and recommend it for people who have never spent a night outside of a building. It's great for families with kids, and some camp-grounds even allow dogs. Years ago I was with a partner who didn't like backpacking or hiking, so we car-camped at night and went our separate ways during the day -- I'd go hiking and she went shopping. Car-camping was the solution to our different preferences.

There are two car-camping options available in the Green Mountain National Forest. One is the developed campground, and there are three of these in the southern section. Hapgood Pond, described in Chapter 6, has 28 sites, and the beautiful pond for swimming. It is located about six miles east of Manchester, then two miles north of Peru on Hapgood Pond Road (at the fork, keep right). This campground offers more than the other two listed below -- the pond, trails, barrier-free campsites, etc. But you will also pay more, and campsites are $13 here for overnights, $5 for day use only.

Greendale Campground is located on the eastern side of the Forest, on the edge of the White Rocks National Recreation Area, near the town of Weston. You can find it by going about 2 miles north of Weston on Route 100, then turning left onto Forest Road 18 for another two miles. It has eleven campsites, pit toilets, and a hand pump for water. The sites are big enough for small trailers and small motorhomes, and the cost is $5 per night. The campground stretches alongside Greendale Brook, a tributary of the West River. From the campground, a hike of about 3 miles is possible on the Greendale Trail which passes a beaver pond and some meadows.

The Red Mill Campground is located on Forest Road 274, about 10 miles east of Bennington and one mile north of Route 9. This campground, which surrounds a wetland that drains into Red Mill Brook, offers 31 campsites, pit toilets, and hand water pumps. Most are tent sites, but some can handle small trailers. No electricity is available. The cost is $5 per night. The maximum length of stay at these three developed campgrounds is 14 days, and the season is from Memorial Day through Labor Day.

The second, generally unknown, option offers fewer amenities to car-campers, but you can do it nearly anywhere in the Green Mountain National Forest. What's called "dispersed camping" is done on pull-outs off the many miles of forest road that run through the Forest. Some roads, such as Forest Road 71 in Somerset, have long stretches of flat land where people park their campers, vans, or pickups with caps. Then they set up a portable picnic table, light up a barbecue, and turn on a battery powered radio, or maybe even a television. The Forest Service does not provide any amenities, including trash cans or pit toilets, but they let these people car-camp for as long as 14 days in any one place. And, there are no permits necessary for this sort of outdoor experience. This kind of freedom, which comes with its own set of problems, is rare in the east. It reminds me of the situation a few decades ago in some of the western National Forests.

I've noticed that certain people seem to be living in the Green Mountain National Forest. I've been told by locals and insiders that some people stay at one "dispersed" site for two weeks, then simply move to another. In the summer of 1998 the Rainbow People descended on the Forest, making it seem like it was 1968. But what they did was, for the most part, legal. The Forest Service even has a flyer of recommended areas to do this kind of car camping. Comparing this situation with camping in the White Mountain National Forest in New Hampshire can cause one to wonder at the bizarre freedom afforded in Vermont.

Those interested in car-camping should also know about Grout Pond (see Chapter 6), and two State parks, Woodford and Emerald Lake. Woodford State Park is a 400-acre Vermont State park right off Route 9 that offers campsites, showers, swimming, and playgrounds. It has a hiking trail that penetrates the edge of the George D. Aiken Wilderness (see Chapter 4). Emerald Lake State Park is located in the narrowest section of the Valley of Vermont in East Dorset, near the White Rocks National Recreation Area. Mount Dorset towers above its campsites, lean-tos, and short hiking trails. The lake offers swimming, and boat rentals are available.

Woodford State Park
>142 State Park Road, Woodford, VT 05201,
>802/447-7169 (summer)
>802/483-2001 (winter)

Emerald Lake State Park
>374 Emerald Lake Land, East Dorset, VT 05253-9788
>802/362-1655 (summer)
>802/483-2001 (winter)

Finger Lakes National Forest

In western New York state, in Schuyler and Seneca counties, is the 13,232 acre Finger Lakes National Forest, a large land holding that is administered by Green Mountain National Forest. This area, originally called the Hector Land Use Area, was acquired in 1954 and became a part of the National Forest system in 1983. It is located on a high ridge between Seneca and Cayuga Lakes in western New York State.

The Federal government acquired most of the land parcels that make up the Finger Lakes National Forest during the Depression. This was a time when the local farmers were doing poorly, suffering from soil depletion and competition with Midwest farming. The government bought one hundred farms between 1938 and 1941. Soil stabilization was promoted and the former cropland was converted to a grazing area for cattle. While the area has been opened to various kinds of recreation, the Department of Agriculture still issues permits to local farmers that allow their cattle to graze there. Horseback riding, camping, and berry picking are popular activities. Two miles of the Finger Lakes Trail passes through the area. For more information: *Finger Lakes National Forest,* 5218 State Route 414, Hector, NY 14841, (607) 546-4470.

Contacting the Green Mountain National Forest

Rules and regulations for public use of the National Forest may be obtained from the Manchester Ranger District office on Routes 11 and 30 just east of Manchester. Forest maps, topographic maps, sketch maps, informative brochures, and general information may also be obtained at this office which is open daily 9-5.

Manchester Ranger District
　　　　2538 Depot Street
　　　　Routes 11 & 30
　　　　Manchester Center, VT 05255-9419
　　　　802-362-2307 VOICE/TTY

Information may also be obtained from the Forest Supervisor's Office in Rutland which administers both the southern and northern sections of the Forest.

Forest Supervisor's Office
　　　　231 North Main Street
　　　　Rutland, VT 05701-2417
　　　　802-747-6700 TTY 802/747-6765

Chapter 2

The Origins and History of Southern Vermont

The Geology of the Southern Green Mountains

The Green Mountains in southern Vermont are composed of the oldest rock in New England. A geological map of the state of Vermont will show a long band of 900 million-year-old Precambrian rock extending from the Massachusetts border to a point just north of Rutland. Interestingly, the dimensions of this band are approximately the same as the publicly owned land in the southern section of the Green Mountain National Forest (the area covered by this guide), so the title of this book could have been "Hiking on New England's Most Ancient Rocks." The White Mountains of New Hampshire are young in comparison to the Green Mountains, which are in turn younger than the rock of the truly ancient Adirondacks.

While the actual sequence of mountain-building events that created the Green Mountains is not known with absolute certainty, the following blow-by-blow description is probably fairly close to what actually happened. The Appalachian Mountains, the larger chain to which the Green Mountains belong, are the product of a series of collisions of land masses. Geologists have determined that the continents are actually large plates that float over the denser and more plastic materials that lie deep beneath the surface of the earth. Over time, the mountains and higher areas of these plates are broken down by water and wind, and sediments are washed into the surrounding ocean. These sediments then settle on the part of the plate that lies underwater. Eventually, these deposits of sand and silt will accumulate to great depths and become pressed together, forming sedimentary rocks.

These continental plates are slowly but constantly changing positions, and from time to time they bump into each other. It takes millions of years for two plates to go through a cycle of collision and separation. With each collision, the sedimentary deposits at their edges become folded and compressed, a process that normally results in the creation of mountains. The movements of the plates are extremely slow, but since they are so huge they have enough inertia to fold layers of sediments lying under water and shove them thousands of feet into the air. This is why sea fossils, such as those of the Burgess Shale, are sometimes found high up on mountains. In the case of the Green Mountains, a plate collision involving the North American and Eurasian plates that happened over a billion years ago created a belt of ancient metamorphic rock (compressed and cooked sedimentary rock).

Subsequent plate collisions, at least two of them, folded more rock and added land to the east. The oldest rock, the product of the earlier collision, is now located well to the west of the edge of the plate. And that old rock, mostly schist and gneiss that was formerly on the edge of the continent and bashed up by a collision with Eurasia, is now the core of the southern Green Mountains.

The Taconic Mountains

Just to the west of the main range of the Green Mountains is the Taconic range. Between the two is a narrow strip of fertile land called the Valley of Vermont. Bennington, Manchester, and Rutland are located here, on top of rocks that are completely different from those of the Green Mountains and the rocks of the Taconics. There are thus three distinct geological zones that must be considered in a discussion of the southern section of the Green Mountain National Forest; the ancient core rock of the Green Mountains, the rocks on the floor of the Valley of Vermont, and the rocks of the Taconic Mountains that sit upon the latter.

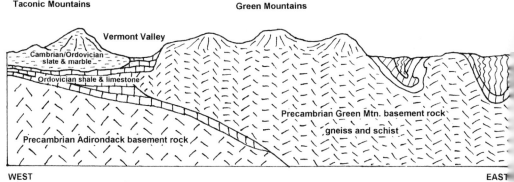

Generalized Cross Section of Southern Vermont

The rocks of the Taconic Mountains are mostly slates and marbles, which suggests that they originated as ocean sediments, deposited by rivers draining the continental plate. What's really strange about the Taconic Mountains is that they are composed of rock that is older than the rock they stand on. And they seem to be standing upside down. How did they get there? Modern geologists say they are composed of rock that was pushed up and over the Green Mountain core by the collision of plates. Support for this theory comes from the comparison of rock types. The Green Mountains are composed, for the most part, of Precambrian gneiss and schist. The much younger slates and marbles of the Taconics are similar to those of the area southeast of the Green Mountains.

Some geologists have suggested that the Taconics are actually the younger rocks that once capped the older Green Mountain core rocks. According to this view, they apparently slipped off and landed west of the main Green Mountain range. There have been other equally odd explanations. The fact is that the Taconic Mountains are what is called by geologists a klippe, a rock mass that has been relocated and positioned over younger rock. Astute readers will notice that this Taconic orogeny (episode of mountain building) is but the earliest example of a series of boundary issues centered in the southern Green Mountains.

The Valley of Vermont lies between the ancient Green Mountains and the younger Taconics west of them. This valley extends from northern Connecticut, through Western Massachusetts, and up to Rutland, Vermont. Route 7 runs through it. In this section, the Valley is relatively narrow, but north of Rutland it widens into what's known as the Lake Champlain lowland. Geologists tell us that the rock of the Valley of Vermont started as calcium carbonate deposits in an ancient sea. For eons microscopic marine organisms with tiny skeletons lived and died there, their hard remains gradually accumulating to a depth of almost two miles. These remains solidified into limestone. When the continental plates collided again, this ancient sea floor was compressed and uplifted, as were older basement rocks. This mountain-building episode resulted in the formation of the original Taconic Highlands. Continuous pressure from the collision of plates to the east resulted in the transformation of some of the limestone into marble, and the movement of older rocks over younger rocks. The result are today's displaced Taconic Mountains and the exposure of the limestone and marble, which erode faster than the rocks around them, thus creating the Valley of Vermont. The whole story is far more complicated than this, but this summary should give you the basic idea.

Indians and Early Settlers

The land that is now called southern Vermont was formerly inhabited by small groups of Abnaki Indians. A few ancient habitation sites have been uncovered, including the Cloverleaf Site along the Walloomsac River near Bennington. This site, which was occupied some 4,000 years ago, is being excavated by the University of Maine at Farmington and tours of the site are offered (802/447-7391).

Other evidence of Indian occupation has been found throughout the region including the town of Jamaica, which is apparently located on the site of a former Indian village and derives its name from a native word for beaver. This situation, where an English settlement was built where an Indian village once stood, is a common and widespread phenomenon.

31

Few Americans realize the extent to which the white man has built over existing Indian habitation sites and usurped their transportation arteries. Just look at a map of Indian trails and settlements and compare this to a modern road map. Route 103, which connects the Connecticut River valley with Lake Champlain follows, more or less, an original Indian road. Parts of it were once called the Crown Point Road. Thankfully (for the sake of preserving historical tradition), at least some of the early Indian place names have been retained.

We've seen how the Taconic Mountains were displaced from east to west, and how this has confounded the geologists. On the cultural level, similar boundary contests have occurred and are still occurring. Prior to the English invasion, the Abnaki and Iroquois Indians fought over the western side of the territory. The Mahicans, whose territory extended along the upper Hudson to Lake Champlain and into the Berkshires, overlapped the area to some extent as well. The result of these territorial overlaps led to periodic fighting and the limiting of any substantial, permanent habitation sites in what is now the Green Mountain National Forest.

Colonists

It was not until the end of the French and Indian Wars, around 1760, that Vermont became safe for the English Invaders. During this period, grants for Vermont land were given out by authorities in both New Hampshire and New York. Here's what happened. In the mid-18th century, King George II of England gave Governor Benning Wentworth of New Hampshire power over the real estate west of New Hampshire to a point about 40 miles east of the Hudson River. The towns that originated from Wentworth's pen are called the New Hampshire grants. At the same time, the King gave similar land-granting rights to the Governor of New York, whose range extended from New York State to the Connecticut River. The lands in Vermont originally given by that state are called the New York patents. Adding further to the confusion were the claims that France made upon the region, which were asserted in the bloody French and Indian Wars. In some ways, this confounding and impossible boundary situation actually caused Vermont to come into being as a separate entity.

The first settlers in Vermont came from New Hampshire. Bennington, in the far west of today's Vermont, was first settled in 1761 and was named for the governor of New Hampshire. Among the first settlers in the region was Ethan Allen, illustrious leader of the Green Mountain Boys.

Troubles began when the New York government at Albany chose to exercise authority over Vermont by claiming Bennington. The attempt turned into a fiasco. About 300 armed men were sent, only to be routed by the Vermonters who "spanked" them with birches and sent them back. The Green Mountain Boys became known in New York as the "Bennington Mob." However, the outbreak of hostilities between England and the Colonies halted this in-fighting and created an opportunity for the Green Mountain Boys to distinguish themselves as competent, respected rebels. They immediately took Fort Ticonderoga from the British. The cannons from this fort were dragged all the way to Boston where they were aimed at the British fleet. The fleet got the message, left Boston, and sailed to New York.

Vermont was not one of the thirteen original colonies. During the War for Independence and shortly thereafter it was, in fact, its own republic that had a constitution, issued currency, and granted land. Its capital shifted over time between Bennington, Arlington, Manchester, Windsor, and several other Vermont towns. The Republic of Vermont's first post office opened in 1789 in Bennington. In 1791 Vermont became the 14th state.

The Towns of the Southern Green Mountains

Hikers visiting the Green Mountain National Forest will pass through some of the numerous Vermont towns on their way to trailheads. There's some very interesting history to be found throughout the region, and knowing something about the towns will add much to a trip there. The following sketches are given in an order that has been determined by topography.

The Towns of Route 7

Located just north of the Massachusetts border is the small town of **Pownal**, named for Pownall brothers, Thomas and John, who served as British governors, administrators, and commissioners. A natural feature near the town is the cascade known as The Weeping Rocks. The name stems from a Mahican prophesy that said the tribe would not be defeated by their enemies until the rocks wept. In 1668 the Mahicans were defeated by the Mohawks at these cascades.

Bennington, first settled in 1672, is a major town in southern Vermont. New Hampshire's land-granting governor, Benning Wentworth, named the town for himself, by himself. Much history was made here, and names like Ethan Allen, the Bennington Mob, and the Green Mountain Boys conjure up images of the kind of rugged individualism that has been associated with the state of Vermont itself.

A major battle of the American Revolution was fought just outside of Bennington. Near the monument for this battle is the town's historic district, and in back of it is Mount Anthony. This mountain may have taken its name from a local person, though the Abnaki name is Askaskwigek, meaning green grass-covered mountain.

The story of the Battle of Bennington deserves telling, for it is one of the few instances in military history of improvised troops beating professional soldiers. One important detail should be mentioned -- the battle actually took place just over the New York line near the tiny town of Walloomsac. Here's what happened.

The British war strategy during the American Revolution (more accurately named "The War for Independence") was to cut New England off from the rest of the colonies by taking over the north-south Hudson River and Lake Champlain corridor. British General John Burgoyne, "Gentleman Johnny," was pushing south from Canada down the Champlain Valley with a large army and many camp followers. His forces took Fort Ticonderoga and Mount Independence without much trouble. Around the end of July, 1777, he stopped at Fort Edward on the Hudson, just short of where he intended to join forces with the British in Albany. He was confident that he would be successful in cutting off the colonies, but he needed supplies and sent a Colonel Baum out to Bennington and "Brattle Borough" to get supplies and take hostages.

Meanwhile, on the American side, Colonel John Stark of New Hampshire, who had become disgusted with Congress for not promoting him and had returned to his home state, was called back into service to help deal with this situation. Leading the New Hampshire forces, he marched west and reached Bennington on August 9th. On August 12th, Baum started marching for Bennington with a group of about 800 that included Hessian mercenaries, a number of Indians and Canadians, and many camp followers, musicians, and servants. Stark's spies reported this movement on the 14th and Stark, with a force of 1,800 ragged farmers and woodsmen, moved east to meet Baum's troops. At Sancoick Mills near Walloomsac, New York, Stark's vanguard fired on Baum's men, sniping from the woods. After more skirmishing and bridge burning, Stark withdrew. It rained on the next day so there was no fighting. On the 16th, a clear but very hot day, Stark said, "We beat them today or Molly Stark's a widow." (Route 9, the Molly Stark Highway, was named after John's wife.) The fight started around three in the afternoon.

Baum took up a defensive position for the attack that was led by Stark and Seth Warner, a Green Mountain Boys leader. Immediately, Baum's Indians and Canadians ran. His defenses were hit hard with guns, and they soon ran out of ammunition. From their entrapment, Baum and his Hessians attacked the Americans with swords, trying to cut their way out. But Baum was shot and soon., the Hessian forces were smashed.

Meanwhile, an officer named Breymann, who was said to be a brutal drillmaster, was marching 550 Germans to Baum's aid. He wasn't moving very quickly, though. He was dragging cannons through mud and stopping periodically to make his men practice drills. Approaching the battlefield, he ran into fire from the Americans, who were by this time disorganized and tired from the heat of the day. Stark's recommendation was to fall back and regroup to meet this new German advance, but Seth Warner argued to stay and fight. After some more fighting, now with heavy cannons, the Hessians were able to advance. Things were not looking so good for the Americans. But then a company of 350 fresh Green Mountain Boys arrived from Manchester. They turned the tide and by sunset it was a rout. The Americans were victorious.

After the battle, in which 200 of the enemy were killed, Stark took 600 prisoners. On the American side, 30 were killed, 40 wounded. The dead soldiers of both sides were buried in the Old Burying Grounds in Bennington. This battle was the beginning of the end for Burgoyne (his complete loss was cemented with the victory of Arnold and Gates at Saratoga). The Bennington Battle Monument, which commemorates this historic event, is 306 feet high and located on the hill where the storehouse that Burgoyne planned to take once stood. It was dedicated in 1891 and was for a time the highest battle monument in the world.

Arlington is another very old Vermont town, first settled in 1763, and certainly more "Vermont" than Manchester. The landscape pictured on the Vermont State Seal is derived from a view here, looking west. The mountains just west of Arlington include The Ball, named for its rounded shape, Grass Mountain, which was once grass-covered, and Spruce Peak which is over 3,000 feet in elevation. Big Spruce Mountain, west of The Ball, is just over 2,300 feet. At Arlington, the Batten Kill river turns west and eventually flows into the Hudson River.

Manchester is three towns in one, Manchester Center, Manchester Village, and Manchester Depot. The first is affluent, traditional Vermont, the second, once known as Factory Point, is a town of outlets for tourists, and the third is linked to the forest industries.

On Prospect Rock, overlooking Manchester

The sidewalks in Manchester are made of sawed marble slabs, marble being a commercial product of this region of Vermont. This town was also the unofficial capital (among others) of the Republic of Vermont. In fact, the first Council of Safety met here. Manchester has long been a fashionable resort. This was the summering place for the wives of Presidents Lincoln and Grant, and Presidents Taft and Theodore Roosevelt also visited the town.

Hikers will know Manchester for its massive mountain, Mount Equinox, which rises high above the town just west of it. Mt. Equinox is not one of the Green Mountains, it's a Taconic. At 3,852 feet, it is the second highest summit in southern Vermont and is clearly recognizable from most directions by both its huge mass and the building on its summit. This mountain is very high when you consider vertical relief, for Manchester lies at only about 750 feet of elevation. How it came to be named Equinox is not clear. Some say it was named by Colonel Partridge, a state Surveyor General in the 1820s, who just happened to be surveying it at the time of the autumnal equinox. But a map from 1796 shows the mountain already had that name. One suggestion is that the name is an English distortion of an Indian word. Ekwanok means a "place of fog," or "place of the woman." A number of smaller, individual peaks are nearby including Deer Knoll and Little Equinox. Mother Myrick Mountain, 3,290 feet high, is named for a farm woman who lived on its slope in the 18th century.

Manchester also includes two hamlets, one called Rootville. Those who hike to Prospect Rock will know this name because the trailhead is on Rootville Road. It was named for the Root family in the 19th century. Another hamlet is Richville, on the banks of the Batten Kill. Lye Brook (see Chapter 4, page 76) flows into the Batten Kill, it being named for an early potash-making business. Bourn Brook flows through Downer Glenn over which perches Prospect Rock. It was named for a family made famous by the Bourn Murder Trial of 1819. In 1812 a Manchester man named Russell Colvin suddenly disappeared, right after an argument with Jesse and Stephen Bourn. The Bourns were arrested, tried, and found guilty of murder. They were to be hanged in 1820, but just before the scheduled execution, it was discovered that Colvin was alive and well, and living in New Jersey.

Just north of Manchester is **East Dorset**, a quiet village at the base of Mount Aeolus, or Green Peak. Marble quarried here as early as 1812 was used to build the New York City Public Library. Mt. Aeolus is part of Dorset Mountain, another multi-peaked formation in the Taconic range. This mountainous mass begins with Owls Head and Mount Aeolus in the south and ends with Dorset Peak in the north, 3,804 feet high. Both Dorset and Mount Equinox are among the summits coveted by peakbaggers who climb New England's hundred highest peaks. Just north of East Dorset is Emerald Lake, the main feature of Emerald Lake State Park, and formerly known as Dorset Pond. It lies in the Valley of Vermont where the Green Mountains on the east drop down to within a few hundred feet of the Taconic Mountains on the west. Here is the narrowest gap between these two ranges.

On the southwest side of the Dorset Mountain mass is the town of **Dorset**, and a few miles beyond it (off Route 315 in Rupert) is the Merck Forest and Farmland Center. This center is a community-supported, non-profit environmental education organization that was established by the late George Merck, former president of the pharmaceutical firm. Merck created a board of trustees to manage the original 2,000 acres deeded to the organization, which is not supported by (and has nothing to do with) Merck Pharmaceuticals. Today, the 3,100 acre Merck Forest and Farmland Center contains 28 miles of hiking trails, campsites (including cabins and shelters), and a visitor center. Environmental and farming programs are presented year round. For information, contact Merck Forest & Farmland Center, PO Box 86, Rupert, VT 05768, 802-394-7836.

The next town north from Manchester on Route 7 is **Danby**, famous for its marble and Silas Griffith, Vermont's first millionaire. You'll find the S.L. Griffith Memorial Library here, and also Griffith's house, which is now the Silas Griffith Inn. Griffith was a lumber baron and made his fortune from the Green Mountains just east of Danby. Closer to town are the quarries of the Vermont Marble Company. Nearby Dorset Peak was the source of the marble for the Supreme Court building in D.C.

The town of **Mount Tabor** lies on the other side of Route 7 from Danby. It was originally named Harwich, a name that was given by a New York grant and serves as a reminder of New York's influence in Vermont's early history. The town was renamed by popular request for Gideon Tabor, a notable citizen who served in the Revolutionary War. He also served as a town moderator, town clerk, justice of peace, and in the Vermont legislature. On the border with Danby was once a village called Brooklyn, but it later became Griffith because most of the mail passing through was related to the Griffith sawmills, kilns, etc.

The crossroads on Route 7 between Danby and Mount Tabor still have an industrial look. Hikers heading for Little Rock Pond and Big Branch will have to turn here to enter the National Forest. Mount Tabor is mostly part of the National Forest. Of its 27,000 acres, only 3,000 are privately owned. Greeleys Mills of Mount Tabor once cut wood using water power in what is now known as the Big Branch Recreation Area. Big Branch was once known as Great Branch.

The northernmost town adjacent to the Green Mountain National Forest is **Wallingford**, named after Wallingford, Connecticut, where many of its early settlers came from. The Connecticut town, in turn, was named for Wallingford in Berkshire, England. Wallingford, Vermont, was once known for its production of tools. Located here was the True Temper Tool Factory, manufacturers of hand garden tools. Sugar Hill, just east of town and where one turns off to the White Rocks Recreation Area, is said to be the place where the first maple sugar in Vermont was made. Wallingford Pond was once known as Lake Hiram, named for a man who lived nearby.

The Route 100 Towns

Readsboro, an old industrial town on the Deerfield River, was named for settler John Reade. Over the years it has been spelled Readesborough, Reedsborough, and Reedsberry. The land in the area was originally granted to Major Robert Rogers, of Roger's Rangers. In the center of town is Readsboro Falls, which once supported several sawmills.

West Readsboro became **Heartwellville** in 1852, named for early settler Joseph Hartwell. Nearby Dutch Hill was named for Dutch settlers from New York who lived there. It was once the location of a downhill ski area, the remnants of which are still clearly visible. Between Readsboro and Heartwellville is Lamb Brook, a scene of controversy in the early 1990s. The Forest Service planned to clear-cut parts of the large tract of woodland bounded by Routes 100, 8, 9, and the Harriman Reservoir, but were stopped in court by a coalition of grass roots organizations. No logging has happened there yet and Forest Watch, an environmental organization, has proposed that it become a wilderness area.

Wilmington lies in a junction of valleys and at the junction of Routes 9 and 100. Two northern branches of the Deerfield River come together here as well. Today Wilmington is a tourist town, especially in winter when it caters to the ski crowd who swarm to Mount Snow, many from New York, New Jersey, and Connecticut. Sometimes these visitors are too much for a town with only one stop light. Several times I've been caught in traffic that was backed up for a mile on a Sunday afternoon during ski season. Wilmington once had a hamlet called Mountain Mills, a place where logs arrived to be made into pulp and wood. The creation of the Harriman Dam flooded Mountain Mills so fast that it had to be hastily evacuated. Now it's under water, visible only when the reservoir is down.

Dover was created from the south district of Wardsboro in 1810. Today, **West Dover** is larger and better known than Dover because of the Mount Snow ski resort. The North Branch of the Deerfield River runs through the valley that West Dover lies within, which is now dotted with a strange mix of cows and ski-related businesses.

Up against the mountain range is a narrow strip of land called the Handle. It was once a part of the town of Somerset, but the Mount Snow range (formerly known as Somerset Mountain, and later Mount Pisgah) was a major barrier to communication between these two parts of the town, which grew apart. Somerset wanted to give the land away because everyone living there was focused on Dover anyway. But Dover didn't want it. In 1859 it was given to Stratton and Wilmington, the latter part becoming known as Wilmington Leg or The Handle. It was called this because, like the panhandle of the state of Oklahoma, the thin strip of land stuck out of the main body of Wilmington. Ten years later it became part of Dover. Handle Road still exists and runs right along the lower eastern flanks of the Haystack-Mount Snow range.

Wardsboro is another town with many villages. There's West Wardsboro, South Wardsboro, Wardsboro Center, and a just plain Wardsboro. **West Wardsboro**, where hikers turn west to hike in the Stratton Mountain area, started out as Hammonds Mills in 1832, then changed names in 1846. **Jamaica** and **Bondville** are two towns along the Route 30 corridor, one of the few paved roads that cuts through the Green Mountains. Jamaica is said to be the site of an ancient Indian village. Bondville is in the shadow of Stratton, both the mountain itself and the giant ski resort.

Londonderry stands on the banks of the West River at a gully that is perfect for a sawmill. The area was originally patented in 1770 by the New York governor to Captain James Rogers (the younger brother of Robert Rogers) and 22 other veterans of the French and Indian wars. The area was then called Kent. James Rogers somehow convinced the other 22 men to transfer their interest in the area to him. Rogers was living at the time in Londonderry, New Hampshire, which was named for Londonderry, Ireland, which the Rodgers Scottish-Protestant descendants had emigrated from before leaving for America. Rogers then moved, along with some neighbors and friends, to Kent. But when the War for Independence began, he sided with the Crown and went off to join Burgoyne's army. For this action, his property was confiscated by the Republic of Vermont. This was unfortunate for his neighbors, who now had no clear title to their homes, and they asked the Republic of Vermont for some resolution. In 1780 a new charter was issued and the name was changed to Londonderry, after their old home town in New Hampshire.

To the east of Londonderry and north of Route 11 is Lowell Lake, formerly Derry Pond, one of the higher lakes at 1,300 feet and very beautiful. It was the site of the Lowell Lake House, a summer resort. Just south of the lake, on the other side of Route 11, is the Magic Mountain ski area, the cut slopes of which are visible from the summit of Bromley Mountain. Magic is not the real name of the mountain, which is just shy of 3,000 feet, that supports this open-again, closed-again ski area. Glebe Mountain is the true name, and it is not within the boundaries of the Green Mountain National Forest.

Weston is located very near the source of the West River. The Abnaki name for this river is Wantastiquet, which means "at the river's source." Wantastiquet is also the name of the high mountain just east of Brattleboro, on the New Hampshire side of the Connecticut River. It's at this point that the West River empties into the Connecticut. The West River drops 2,000 feet in 40 miles, draining an area of 430 square miles. Its flooding in 1927 led to the construction of the Townshend Dam on Route 30 near Townshend.

The Hill Towns

Searsburg is a tiny town high in the mountains between Wilmington and Bennington on Route 9, the Molly Stark Trail. Before the road was Route 9 and the Molly Stark Trail, it was known as the Searsburg and Windham Turnpike, an early toll road. Today, Searsburg is famous for snowmobiles and wind generation. From many high spots in the southern Green Mountains, you can see the family of wind turbines that have been built on a high ridge within the boundaries of this town. The official name of this installation is the Searsburg Wind Power Facility, owned and operated by Green Mountain Power. The project was completed in 1997 and is the largest wind power plant in the east. It's also specially designed to handle the Vermont winter. The blades are painted black to absorb sunlight and melt ice and snow. The turbines produce electricity in winds of over 10 miles per hour and reach a plateau of power production in 30 mph winds. Above that speed, the blades are pitched to deflect the higher winds and prevent damage to the units. These are huge wind generators that stand 132 feet above the ground, not counting the extension of the rotor blades at the top of their cycle. The energy they generate, 6 megawatts, is said to provide energy to 2,000 average Vermont households.

Somerset is almost a ghost town and a long way from anywhere. It never had a village center, even though it had a population of 300 in 1850. A post office did exist here from 1870 to 1916, in a private home, but the town was disenfranchised in 1937. Today it is mostly a part of the Green Mountain National Forest or U.S. Generating, which acquired the New England Power Company and manages the Somerset Reservoir and its drainage to the Harriman Reservoir. The dispersed camping area called the Landing Strip was once a real landing strip for small planes. During the summer it is an end-to-end lineup of small trailers, SUVs, pickup trucks, and people sitting under temporary canopies grilling meat on barbecues, and maybe even watching a portable television -- a rather questionable way to enjoy the great outdoors, in my opinion.

Woodford is said to be the highest village in Vermont. It is indeed a highly elevated town with 20 summits over 2,000 feet, including Bald Mountain, Maple Hill, Hagar and Harmon Hills (named for locals), Prospect Mountain (named for its view), and The Elbow, which is elbow-shaped. Iron deposits were discovered here long ago and were used to make anchors for use on American gunboats.

The town was possibly named for a General Woodford, a British army officer during the French and Indian wars. It might also have been named for Woodford in Essex, England, which was a wooded place, like Woodford, Vermont. Woodford City was the actual hill town, while Woodford Hollow was the business center. This later settlement was sometimes called The Hollow or Dunville Hollow because it was located near the confluence of City Stream and Walloomsac Brook. Slab City was yet another name, one coined during the lumber era.

Located in the southeastern corner of Woodford is the George D. Aiken Wilderness Area. Here, in two low-lying areas, is the source of the West Branch of the Deerfield River. The Aiken Wilderness is a mostly non-descript, high wetland full of beaver ponds, except for two names that appear on many maps. Beaver Meadow was said to be grassland when the first settlers arrived, and Camp Meadow was where an early surveying party was said to have camped.

Today Woodford is the host to winter sport enthusiasts of two types. Cross-country skiers find the Prospect Mountain Ski Area a wonderful place to ski, a place where snow covers the ground for months. The grooming here is excellent and the lodge cozy. At one time Prospect Mountain was a downhill ski area, and later on it was both downhill and cross-country. Competition from Mount Snow/Haystack led to the closing of the downhill portion around 1989. The abundance of snow is also the reason why Woodford is "snowmobile central" in winter. People in high-clearance trucks or SUVs pulling large trailers containing two or more snowmobiles come here all winter long, but especially on weekends. Then, more often then not, the two National Forest parking areas on Route 9 are full. Several companies offer snowmobile tours through the backcountry. No doubt much petroleum is burned up in Woodford every winter.

Glastenbury was part of a New Hampshire grant, granted on August 20th, 1761, the same day as several other nearby towns. It was spelled Glossenburry, but later the spelling was changed to match the English spelling of the town in Somerset, England. Glastenbury was an ill-omened town. Farming was not easy and the town attracted few settlers. In 1791 there were only 34 people living there. When it was incorporated in 1834, the population had reached only 50. Glastenbury's only resource was timber, but this allowed it to have a period of prosperity after the Civil War, one that was based around charcoal manufacturing. A major part of Glastenbury's problems was that a rail connection to Bennington involved a major climb of 9 miles to the southernmost part of the town. The road's grade was a rise of 250 feet per mile, said to be the steepest in the country.

Business flourished for a while and big charcoal kilns shipped 30,000 bushels of charcoal every month. The boom was over by 1889, though some tourism carried on in the form of a hotel and casino. In 1898 a flood wiped out the railroad and by 1937 the town was disenfranchised. In 1950 there was one resident. Today Glastenbury is a ghost town, with only a few summer residents coming to Fayville, the only hamlet left. Recently, a 4,000-acre tract of private land in this area was acquired by the Trust for Public Land in New England and then transferred to the Forest Service. Groups such as the TPL are vital in preserving wilderness and staving off development and business that should be located elsewhere.

The town of Glastenbury is also associated with mystery, not surprising since it is so remote. For example, there is the case of the Bennington Monster, a strange creature that was said to have attacked a stagecoach traveling from Woodford in 1892. The creature, described as gigantic, knocked over the coach, roared, and stomped back into the woods. Some have suggested this creature is a Vermont species of Bigfoot. Other strange things have happened in this area as well. UFO activity has been reported, and between 1945 and 1950, at least five people, and possibly as many as nine, have completely vanished in the Glastenbury wilderness.

Stratton, the town, never had too many residents, but being on the road between West Wardsboro and Arlington, it was far from being a wilderness like Glastenbury or Somerset. It was probably named after the town of Stratton in Cornwall, England. For the most part, though, Stratton was a timber town and it boomed between 1830 and 1880. A prominent Stratton family back then was the Grout family. The name has survived in Grout Job, which is the old clearing where the LT/AT parking lot is located, and in Grout Pond. Stratton Pond, the watery gem of the area, was originally known as North Pond or Jones Pond.

The town of Stratton lies along the Arlington-West Wardsboro Road, known locally as Kelly Stand Road. On this road, about 6.5 miles west of Route 100, is a gravel turnoff to a stone marker that commemorates the day when 15,000 people came out to hear the great orator Daniel Webster. This was on July 7th and 8th, 1840. Webster had been asked to speak about the upcoming primary elections in several southern Vermont towns, but he decided to choose a central spot and give one speech. His choice was a 300-acre clearing in the tiny town of Stratton, midway between Manchester, Bellows Falls, Bennington, and Brattleboro. His politics? Webster was a Whig and was seeking votes for William Henry Harrison to run against the incumbent Democrat Martin Van Buren. Harrison got the nomination, won the presidency, and appointed Webster Secretary of State.

Peru is a well-groomed town on high ground. The New Hampshire Grant of October 13th, 1761, dubbed it Brumley at first, then Bromley. The name was changed to Peru in 1804, supposedly for better public relations (It was thought that an association with the wealth of South America would make the town more appealing). Today, the name Bromley remains only as the name of the famous ski mountain. The population of Peru peaked in the 1840s at 600. The post office in the little town is the original post office built in 1815. Diane Keaton's movie "Baby Boom" was filmed in Peru. Peru's boundaries extend to Mad Tom Brook and Griffith Lake, formerly called Buffum Pond. Among its most prominent families are the Hapgoods, for which Hapgood State Forest and Hapgood Pond are named. Styles Peak was named for the Peru family that owned land near it.

The Railroads and the Power Company

In the late 19th century, southern Vermont was where some of the last large tracts of virgin timber stood, saved from the Industrial Revolution by their remoteness and lack of easy transportation. But in 1884 a corporation called the Deerfield Valley Railroad was formed to connect the Fitchburg Railroad (later the Boston and Maine) in Massachusetts, via the Hoosac Tunnel to Readsboro, Vermont, which lay just over the Massachusetts border. Locally, the railroad was a boon, and the formerly isolated southern Vermonters were enthusiastic about it. In fact, one of the big issues of the day was how far the railroad would extend. In 1886 the corporation's name was changed to the Hoosac Tunnel & Wilmington Railroad Company, a.k.a. the HT&W (affectionately known as the Hoot, Toot & Whistle).

The railroad's extension to Wilmington came about in 1891, but it was not an easy one to build or to maintain. Hugging cliffs and spanning ravines on trestles, this was one steep rail line that climbed 800 feet in 24 miles. The line mostly followed the course of the Deerfield River, including what is today the bottom of the Harriman Reservoir. An industrial area grew up along this line just outside of Wilmington and below a dam on the Deerfield. It was called Mountain Mills and once boasted a 3-story paper mill and about 300 residents.

The extension of the railroad was only part of this region's history of corporate involvement. Southern Vermont's Green Mountains receive much rainfall, which runs off into rivers like the Deerfield. Following the loggers, hydroelectric entrepreneurs were drawn to the area. The New England Power Company (NEPCo) was the next corporate monster on the scene.

NEPCo began a takeover of the area with land acquisitions and the building of the Somerset Dam in Somerset. A key player in this appropriation of nature was Henry I. Harriman of the New England Power Company who had explored the Deerfield River valley in 1908 and chose Wilmington as a place for a reservoir. In 1920 NEPCO bought the HT&W along with most of the land within the valley of the Deerfield River. Then, with almost total control of the area, NEPCo began to construct the Harriman Dam, a 200-foot high wall that in 1924 was the largest of its kind in the world. The base of the dam is 1,300 feet high and a 14-foot diameter tunnel channels water from it to a powerhouse three miles downstream, which has a generating capacity of 42,000 kilowatts. An interesting feature of the dam is its unique "Glory Hole" spillway, which resembles a morning glory flower during periods of high water.

Upstream from the Harriman Reservoir is the Searsburg Reservoir from which water rushes down in a big black tube to a 5,000 kilowatt power station. The black tube is visible from Route 9, east of Wilmington. Further upstream is the Somerset Reservoir. A number of hiking trails and picnic areas were established in this area by the New England Power Company for day-use only, a few of which are described in Chapter 6.

Let's return to the story of the railroad which formerly occupied the Deerfield Valley, and which was now flooded to create the Harriman Reservoir. The people of Wilmington still wanted their rail connection with the rest of the world. Unfortunately, the new relocation of the HT&W was fraught with problems and NEPCo attempted to sell the people of Wilmington on the idea of a ferry that would carry railroad cars down to the end of the dam where the line would end. Wilmington didn't like the idea and forced the company to restore rail service to the town. In order to do this, switchbacks had to be built to bring the trains to the top of the Harriman Dam, and further north, other major obstacles like a deep gully had to be spanned with trestle.

Meanwhile, logging was declining and very few of the narrow-gauge rail lines were being used. The company that had operated these lines was dissolved in 1923, leaving NEPCo as owners of a defunct rail network. Ultimately, NEPCo wasn't really interested in running railroads and so in 1926 it sold most of its holdings. The very next year brought flooding and mudslides that ruined parts of the HT&W line. Repairs on a long trestle were eventually made, but meanwhile the bus service for passengers between Wilmington and the Hoosac Tunnel, that had begun during the interim, had caught on. From then on, the HT&W handled only freight.

In 1936 a big spring runoff washed out the same trestle again, and this was the last straw for the line's owners. The railroad was sold, the line was shortened to Readsboro, and the line north to Wilmington was abandoned. Service continued on the remaining eleven miles until 1971. Today, hikers and cross-country skiers can enjoy the Harriman Trail, the former route of the railroad to Wilmington.

The Ski Industry

The downhill ski industry in southern Vermont has become an integral part of the region's economy -- and not just in the winter. The ski areas are now promoting themselves as four-season destinations and anchors for year-round tourism. For the purposes of this book, the important difference between downhill and cross-country ski areas is the extent to which they dominate the landscape and shape policies that affect hikers. Hikers should learn about the downhill skiing industry, even if they aren't comfortable with some of their practices. (Please don't assume I'm against downhill skiing; I enjoy the sport and have skied all four areas described below. I'm also an enthusiastic cross-country skier.)

Since the 1930s, downhill or alpine skiing has become an established activity in the southern Green Mountains, an area that receives about 300 inches of snow each winter. Today there are four major ski areas, two of them under the same ownership, and they conduct what seems to be a fairly brisk business during the winter season. The result is that four major mountains have been appropriated for intensive recreation, their summits have been built on, and their slopes shaved to accommodate herds of humans equipped to defy gravity. The Long Trail/Appalachian Trail passes over two of these summits, Stratton and Bromley, and for many hikers, the proximity to developed ski areas is disturbing. From a hiker's perspective, mechanical intrusions into the wilderness ruins the experience of nature on her own terms. It's true, ski areas are not very pretty for most of the year.

The good news is that most of the ski slopes face *away* from the heart of the National Forest. Haystack and Mount Snow are on the east face of the easternmost ridge, looking towards Route 100. Stratton's ski trails are on the northern and lower peak of that mountain and face toward Bondsville and Route 30. Bromley Ski Area covers half of Bromley Mountain and faces south to Stratton. Its ski trails are most visible from the ski trails of Stratton, and vice versa. There's also Magic Mountain in Londonderry, just outside the boundaries of the National Forest. Its slopes are almost entirely hidden, except from the summit of Bromley. Overall, the placement of the ski areas in the southern Green Mountains works for hikers and connoisseurs of wilderness vistas. It could be much worse.

Bromley was the first ski area on the scene. Its founder was Fred Pabst, a member of the Pabst beer family. In 1936 he opened up a lower part of Bromley Mountain (what is today the parking area) to skiers, offering them a slope and a tow rope. Bromley became popular in part because it was on a major road, the Peru-Manchester highway. By 1948, after some extensive clearing, Pabst had opened up a lot more of the mountain. The removal of stumps and boulders and the seeding of newly cut trails allowed for skiing with relatively little snow. (In my opinion, Pabst was a very creative trail designer. Some of Bromley's trails, with their curves and humps, are almost works of art.)

During the 1950s Bromley was a major ski area, in the same league as Stowe and Pico. But by the end of the 50s, as state-supported road building was allowing access to more remote ski areas like Killington and Stratton, Bromley suddenly experienced some heavy competition. Pabst sold Bromley in 1971 and it has since been sold several times. Today, Bromley is advertised as "Vermont's Sun Mountain" because of its south-facing slopes. An alpine slide keeps Bromley open for business in summer.

The **Stratton Mountain** ski area was a corporate project right from the beginning. The idea for it began early in 1948 with Malvine Cole, a race swimmer from Washington, D.C., who bought a cabin in the area. She found the area too lonely and thought a ski area would bring in some excitement. A number of supporters, including novelist Pearl Buck, pooled their resources to get such a project going. During the years that followed, the investment project snowballed, some top skiers were brought in as consultants and instructors, and by 1961 the construction work began. On the ground level, Stratton had two things going for it. First was the fact that the land it was being built upon was private land, not land subject to the restrictions of the National Forest. And secondly, the state funded a road right to the ski area from Bondville. Skiing at Stratton started on December 29th, 1961.

Today Stratton is immense. It has 90 trails, an 8-person gondola to the top, and a base area with its own clock tower, not to mention hives of condos and second homes. Hikers climbing Stratton from the south via the LT/AT will have to walk the half mile trail to the top of the gondola lift to see what I'm talking about. Thankfully, the view from the south summit, even from the tower, gives few clues as to what lies behind and under the mountain's north nose.

The Summit of Mt. Snow

Mount Snow, the largest ski resort in the world in the early 1960s, now occupies the entire eastern and northern faces of a large mountain originally called Mount Pisgah or Somerset Mountain. It was the fact that the area below it was farmed by Ruben Snow that led to the name change, not just the more obvious marketing advantage. Walter Schoenknect, who had earlier opened Mohawk Mountain ski area in Connecticut, bought Snow's land in 1953 and managed to open it to skiing on December 12, 1954. By 1958 he had expanded the original seven trails to 32, built a 3-story summit lodge, and installed an open-air, heated swimming pool at the base. Other, even more bizarre additions to the area, like a 350-foot geyser, came in the years following. In 1963 Schoenknect asked the Atomic Energy Commission to detonate a bomb underground so as to create a crater for bowl skiing. This, fortunately, didn't happen. After four snowless winters in the early 1970s, and an oil crisis that kept gasoline prices high, Mount Snow went bankrupt and was taken over by a bank. It was later purchased by the owner of Killington Ski Area.

While Mount Snow was growing, two other smaller ski areas opened on the same Haystack-Mount Snow ridge just to the south. Carinthia Ski Area was right next to Mount Snow and was absorbed by it in 1986. More recently, the Mount Snow empire was acquired by American Skiing Company which owns several other large resorts in the Northeast and the West. Haystack, which opened independently in 1964, was acquired by the owners of Mount Snow in 1994. For my money (and I'm a bargain-seeking Cancer Sun-sign), Haystack is the best deal of all the four ski areas.

Southern Vermont has become a place of four-season tourism. Skiers, mostly downhill but also cross-country, flock to the region all winter long. What might be called "the snowmobile nation" keeps the woods near Woodford buzzing during winter. After a brief rest during spring mud season, Manchester, Bennington, and Wilmington wake up again and summer brings everyone out. Many of the skiers return in the summer with their families. Generally, the men play golf, the kids swim, and the women shop, or sometimes hike. Few people ever see the through-hikers who pass through the area in June and July on their way to Maine. All summer and well into October, day-hikers and one-night backpackers take to the ponds and summits. Fall foliage brings out the leaf peepers in large numbers, the peak occurring around the end of September and the first days of October. As you can see, hikers are but one of many user groups that use the Green Mountains.

Restaurants

Hikers need to fuel up before a hike and re-fuel afterwards. Refined atmospheres and high prices are not what hikers want; they generally prefer real down-to-earth restaurants with reasonable prices, casual atmosphere, and a good variety of foods. Here are some of my favorite eating places -- fast, low-cost restaurants with local flavor that I've visited frequently on my trips to the area.

Dot's Restaurant near the corner of Routes 9 and 100 in Wilmington is a friendly local place serving breakfast, lunch, and dinner. Their chili is great and you can get a beer, too! **Sonny's Cup & Saucer**, on Route 100 less than a mile north of Wilmington, has two curved counters, great atmosphere, and serves breakfast and lunch. The **Blue Ben Diner** on Route 7 just north of downtown Bennington is open early and serves breakfast and lunch, along with some items not normally found at a diner. It gets crowded during normal eating hours. In Manchester Center, try the **Quality Restaurant** on Main Street for basic food (also frequently crowded with tourists). In Londonderry, there's **Stoddards** on the south side of Route 11, which is small, friendly, and interesting. There's an old gas pump just outside the door that says "Eat at Stoddard's, get free gas."

Chapter 3

The Green Mountain Club's *Long Trail*

History of the Long Trail and the GMC

Hiking in the Green Mountain National Forest is more or less synonymous with the Long Trail. Created and maintained by the Green Mountain Club, this trail extends north from the Massachusetts border all the way to Canada. Its route passes near, through, or over the most scenic mountain areas in Vermont. In addition to a well-marked pathway, the Long Trail offers hikers the convenience of camping shelters. Although the Long Trail came first, it shares its route with the Appalachian Trail. In many publications this combined route is referred to as the Appalachian-Long Trails, or AT/LT. The Forest Service signage also employs this convention. *In this guidebook, the precedence of the Long Trail will be repeatedly emphasized by the use of the abbreviation* **LT/AT**.

During the 19th century, few real hiking trails existed in Vermont, or anywhere for that matter. Lacking real trails as we know them today, the hikers of that era (who called themselves "trampers") would bushwack to the top of peaks or follow logging roads to high ledges and summits. Ascutney Mountain, located in eastern Vermont near the Connecticut River, was an exception; it was one of the first mountains in the entire country to have its own trail. A trail was cut there in 1825 to commemorate General Layfayette's visit to the area, though later it became a carriage road. By the early 1900s, many mountains had carriage roads leading to their summits, where a hotel or two may have been built, but real hiking trails were still rare. The creation of the Long Trail changed all that.

It took a teacher who believed that education was incomplete without hiking to make something happen about Vermont's lack of trails. His name was James P. Taylor, and he came up with a brilliant idea, a trail that would span the entire state, linking all of Vermont's major mountains. Taylor had this "vision" while camping in the rain on the densely forested summit of Stratton Mountain. 21 years later, Brenton McKaye conceived the idea of the Appalachian Trail in the same spot, the summit of Stratton.

What is it with Stratton Mountain? It has inspired the creation of two of the world's longest trails, served as a backdrop for Daniel Webster's large audience (described in Chapter 2), and today is home to a huge ski area that dreams about growing up some day to be a Colorado-sized resort. Growth and big ideas seem to find a home on Stratton, the highest peak in the territory described in this book.

Returning to our story of the Long Trail -- Taylor decided that, in order to realize his vision, he first needed to create a club. He spent some time promoting both ideas, the trail and the club, vigorously throughout Vermont. Then he called a meeting of prominent citizens (not specifically hikers) to form the Green Mountain Club that would build and maintain the trail. This historic meeting took place in Burlington on March 11, 1910, at 2 p.m. An astrological chart computed for the "birth" of the GMC appears below.

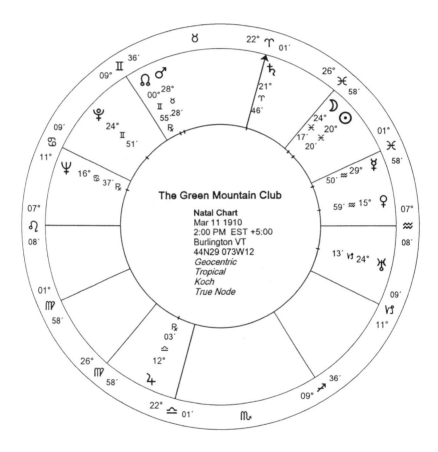

Note that this first official meeting took place during a New Moon in Pisces, the sign of vision and idealism, as well as flexibility and accommodation. The rising sign (Ascendant) is Leo, a sign of marketing and promotion. Saturn was culminating precisely as the meeting convened, a signature of authority and longevity.

Soon after this meeting, "sections" were created, with Burlington being the first one and Bennington the fifth (organized in 1914). Each section was responsible for the building and maintaining of a specific length of the Long Trail.

Taylor was a masterful publicist and he promoted his project as though it were a political campaign. He gave speeches, wrote letters, and befriended the governor. And he got results. A 30-mile section of the "Long Trail" near Mt. Mansfield was built within a year or two. Taylor was a mover and a shaker, but he wasn't personally involved in much of the actual trail work. It took a number of other dedicated supporters, people that were willing to get their hands dirty, to realize his vision.

In southern Vermont, work on the Long Trail began in 1915. An original map that was used to promote the Green Mountain Club shows the trail running over the summits of Haystack and Somerset (Mount Snow) Mountains, then swinging over to Stratton Mountain. From there it continued north by almost the same route that it follows today. The work force necessary to build the Long Trail in Southern Vermont was evidently available and it sprang into action. By 1917, trailwork had linked the Massachusetts border with Killington Mountain. To illustrate how visionary Taylor was, the first idea for the Appalachian Trail was not even conceived until four years after Taylor's achievement, in 1921.

Over the years, the Green Mountain Club has struggled with various intrusions into the wilderness world of the Green Mountains. The GMC has faced the prospect of a mountain motorway that might have been built along the spine of the Green Mountains, and they have struggled with the burgeoning ski industry. More details about this club and its trail can be found in the GMC publication, *Green Mountain Adventure: Vermont's Long Trail.*

Today the club has about 8,000 members, a line of publications, and a headquarters in Waterbury, Vermont. Through largely volunteer work, the Green Mountain Club keeps the Long Trail in pristine condition and educates hikers as to their impact on the forest and mountains. They also work closely with the Forest Service, the stewards of most of the land the trail travels over in southern Vermont. Support of the Green Mountain Club through membership is highly recommended for readers who plan to hike in Vermont.

The Long Trail

The Long Trail is marked with white paint blazes on trees and sometimes on rocks. Important turns are indicated by two of these blazes. At critical junctions, signs are often posted giving mileages between points. Also, registers are placed near some trailheads and hikers should use these to record their names and destinations. This information becomes vital for search and rescue matters, and also serves as an indication of trail use. Parking areas are generally found along the roads crossed by the trail. Some are big enough for only a few cars, so drivers should be especially careful about where and how they park. Some larger parking areas offer a directory of information about the area and its rules and regulations.

The Green Mountain Club also maintains a number of side trails to the LT/AT. These are generally marked in blue and they lead to alternate trailheads. All of them are linked to the LT/AT at one end or the other. The many snowmobile trails that intersect with the Long Trail are distinguished from these side trails by their own markers, and also by their wide pathway.

During peak hiking season, from Memorial Day to Columbus Day, the Green Mountain Club provides caretakers at natural areas that are heavily used and sensitive to human impact. These caretakers generally live in tents for a week or more at a time, rotating with other caretakers. They keep a sharp eye on what goes on in a given area, they educate hikers, and insure that the area is kept clean. They charge a fee for tent campers and shelter users ($5 a night per person in 1999) and they manage the specific areas designated for camping. While some may find this aspect of the club an intrusion on their freedom, it may be the only way to keep human abuse of natural areas to a minimum. Other options, such as permits, quotas, and periodic closings are far less attractive. Hikers have an obligation to keep the land used for hiking in good condition, in this case federal land managed by the Forest Service. The same is expected of other users.

The Long Trail's Route through Green Mountain National Forest

The Long Trail officially begins in southern Vermont at the Massachusetts line at a point deep in the woods. There are two trails that lead to that point, one being the Appalachian Trail, which comes in from North Adams, Massachusetts. Going this way, it is 3.8 miles from Route 2 to the Long Trail, and parking can be a problem (see the *Long Trail Guide*).

The other approach utilizes the Pine Cobble Trail from Williamstown. This trail first leads to Pine Cobble, a series of open ledges and blueberry fields. The Pine Cobble Trail continues northward for another half mile to meet the Appalachian Trail. The total distance from the Pine Cobble Trail trailhead to the Long Trail is 3.2 miles.

Pine Cobble is an interesting area and a fine introduction to the Long Trail. Some years ago I was hiking here and came upon a man who looked like a leprechaun. He had a great beard, big pointed ears, suspenders and a strange hat, and was collecting mushrooms well off the trail in a deep, dark section of the woods. I couldn't resist an attempt at communication with a real leprechaun and soon learned from him all about the delights of the honey fungus, an edible mushroom.

Heading north, the LT/AT reaches the Seth Warner shelter in 2.8 miles. This shelter was named for one of the heroes of the Battle of Bennington and a leader of the Green Mountain Boys. Warner, a calm and steady personality, was respected and trusted by his men, perhaps more so than the fiery and colorful Ethan Allen. He took part in the capture of Fort Ticonderoga in 1775 and later, he and Allen reorganized their own separate armies and together joined the Continental Army. At one point Warner commanded a battalion of seven companies. Unfortunately, his forces were decimated in the battles that took place in Canada. Afterwards, he was made a colonel and ordered to raise a new force. On July 7, 1777, after retreating from Ticonderoga, which Burgoyne had taken back for England, Warner was pursued by the British and badly defeated in a battle at Hubbardton, northwest of Rutland. But a month later his role at the Battle of Bennington helped save the day and set the stage for Burgoyne's big defeat at Saratoga. In 1778 Warner he became a militia general but saw little action. He died at age 41 in 1784. A statue of Seth Warner is located at the head of Monument Avenue in Bennington. Think of him if you stay at the shelter that bears his name.

About one-quarter mile from the Seth Warner Shelter, the LT/AT crosses Mill Road, the county road that connects Stamford and Pownal. The *Long Trail Guide* says that, under good conditions one may be able to drive to this junction. I tried it once but couldn't make it. It was October and there was already some snow on the ground. The potholes were enormous, like small ponds, and my Toyota hit bottom a few times. I wasn't sure where to park so I turned around, and this wasn't easy either. Heading back, and downhill on the snow, I nearly slid off the road. My attempt to drive to the trailhead failed and I still don't really know how close I had come to the LT/AT crossing. Someone with an SUV or a high-clearance pickup truck, however, would probably have no problems on this road.

From Mill Road, the LT/AT climbs a ridge and reaches an elevation of over 3,000 feet from which there are some views. After a descent to a beaver pond, a brook crossing, and some more walking on rolling ridges, the trail heads downhill. A road on the left leads to Sucker Pond. This Bennington reservoir has a road leading to it and some houses on its western end. It's a popular local camp-out area, although camping is not legal there and swimming is prohibited. Another two miles of trail brings one to the Congdon Shelter.

Herbert Wheaton Congdon was a former president of the Green Mountain Club and a strong opponent of the proposed Green Mountain Parkway of the 1930s. Like the Blue Ridge Parkway of the Southern Appalachians, this tourist road would have gouged its way through the heart of these beautiful mountains. We should thank Congdon for his strong stand on this issue, and not James P. Taylor, the founder of the GMC. Taylor, in his other role as a Chamber of Commerce executive, actually supported the plan for the Green Mountain Parkway.

Continuing north, the LT/AT crosses the Old Bennington-Heartwellville Road on which motorized ATVs are allowed during winter. Next, the trail climbs to the pasture-like summit of Harmon Hill, where there is a great view of Bennington and its mountain, Mount Anthony. After a level stretch, the LT/AT makes a very steep descent on rock steps to Route 9, the Molly Stark Highway. There's plenty of parking on both sides of the road here, though the northern parking area is the official one.

The next section of the Long Trail passes through a particularly large tract of undeveloped land. Except for the intense snowmobile activity of winter, the area is virtually empty. No farms, no camps, no paved roads. Only forested ridges, beaver ponds, meadows, streams, and old woods roads. This is the mysterious area known as the Glastenbury Wilderness, said to be the largest area of uninterrupted forest on the entire Long Trail. It is not, however, a true designated Wilderness Area.

From Route 9 the LT/AT climbs 1330 feet in just over two miles to Maple Hill, passing Split Rock and the Melville Nauheim Shelter on the way. The power line cut, which runs just south of the summit, offers some views to the east and west. The high ridge to the east is the Haystack-Mount Snow range. After cresting Maple Hill, the trail descends, crosses Hell Hollow Brook on a bridge and then begins another climb. After attaining the summit of peak 2815 (unnamed summits like this one are often designated by their elevation), the trail drops slightly to a vista called Porcupine Lookout. A short descent to a low point is followed by another climb to peak 3100. On the way, an unmarked side trail on the right leads to Little Pond (see Chapter 6, page 133).

56

According to the *Long Trail Guide*, this "peak 3,100" is Little Pond Mountain. However, the USGS topographic map shows the next mountain north on the trail, at elevation 3,331, to be Little Pond Mountain. Although this mountain is somewhat higher than the 3,100 one, they are connected by a ridge. From the topographic map, it appears that both summits are part of one larger mass. Perhaps Little Pond Mountain could be both of them. My suggestion to the cartographers, whoever they may be, is that the southern summit, peak 3,100, be called *Little* Little Pond Mountain, and that the northern, higher (less little) one retain the name indicated on the map.

The vista from the summit ridge on *Little* Little Pond Mountain that overlooks Little Pond is called Little Pond Lookout. The landscape from this lookout is also little (limited), but it does frame the pond quite nicely. Incidentally, the higher of these two summits is just barely into the boreal zone, while the lower summit doesn't quite make it. Another interesting fact here is that this higher summit is over 1,000 meters. Peakbaggers, take note! (For more information on summits, see Chapter 5, page 87.)

The next stretch of the LT/AT, to Glastenbury Mountain, is long and remote. There's a lookout along the way, and the stone stairs leading to the huge dome which is Glastenbury Mountain make for an abrupt change in foot surface. I've hiked through this area a few times on weekends and, with one exception, did not see a single person. The exception was meeting four 20-something shirtless guys with giant packs hiking at the highest speed possible. I entered into conversation with them, but this did nothing to slow their foot-burning pace. My 50-year old body (and ego) kept up with them for about a mile before I had to slow down. It was quite a workout for me. They were doing the 22-mile loop hike to Glastenbury using the West Ridge Trail (see Chapter 7, page 155) and, apparently, had no time to waste.

Just south of, and below, the summit of Glastenbury Mountain is the Goddard Shelter. This relatively new shelter affords a great view of Mount Greylock in Massachusetts, but it is quite exposed to the west and south. I've never stayed there, but I suspect that it may not be the best shelter to be in during storms that come from the west (as many of them do). Beginning in front of this shelter is the West Ridge Trail, which can be used as a leg in a loop hike going back to Route 9. Ten minutes from the shelter along the LT/AT is the rounded summit of Glastenbury, covered with tall evergreens.

At the actual summit of Glastenbury stands an old fire tower with no roof. Some may find the thin, low walls around the platform a bit unnerving. The view, however, is quite good. All the principle summits of southern Vermont are visible, though they are far away. In between is a vast forest, dotted here and there with tiny ponds and meadows. Below the tower is where a snowmobile trail comes within a few feet of the LT/AT. This lonely, remote summit probably buzzes with motorized recreational activity during the winter months.

From Glastenbury's summit, the LT/AT generally descends, following the ups and downs of the northern extension of the mountain. Near a low point are two shelters. The Kid Gore Shelter is to the east of the trail, and the Caughnawaga Shelter is to the west. Caughnawaga is an Indian word meaning "at the rapids" and was used to refer to the Mohawks who lived in a Christian mission near Montreal. North of these shelters, the trail climbs just to the west of peak 3,412, another unnamed wooded summit of over 1,000 meters. A descent, followed by a passage through a wet area, leads in under five miles to the Story Spring Shelter. The next 2.5 miles of the LT/AT heads east, paralleling the Arlington-West Wardsboro Road, and passing beaver ponds and meadows on the way to the Stratton Mountain parking area on that road. The next seven miles is a "heavy use" section of the LT/AT.

From the parking area on Arlington-West Wardsboro Road, the LT/AT heads north toward Stratton Mountain, which at 3,949 feet is the highest summit in the southern section of the Green Mountain National Forest. For about 1.5 miles the trail wanders up and down, but then, after crossing a dirt road (Forest Road 341), the climb begins. Nowhere is this uphill section truly steep, but it is fairly continuous. Two overlooks are passed on the way to the summit, both looking south over Somerset Reservoir and the Haystack-Mount Snow range.

Like Glastenbury Mountain, Stratton's summit is heavily forested. An old fire tower, this one with a closed observation room, offers excellent views. I've always been amazed at how huge Mount Equinox, looming in the west, looks from Stratton. There used to be a little cabin on the summit of Stratton that was used by the Green Mountain Club caretaker staffed there, but it burned. If you prefer your views from the ground, and don't mind the bizarre apparatus of the ski industry, follow the path on the summit that leads north. Within half a mile you'll come to some clearings on the northern, and lower, summit of Stratton made by the Stratton Mountain Ski Area.

The LT/AT leaves Stratton's summit, heading west and down. You will pass a partially overgrown vista to the west, and farther down, a stream is crossed. After crossing Forest Road 341 again, which is a major snowmobile corridor in winter (Corridor 7), the trail travels through a rolling low area full of beaver ponds and meadows. At a junction with the Stratton Pond Trail, the LT/AT turns north again and passes alongside the eastern shoreline of this beautiful pond. A bridge over an inlet here passes near a healthy stand of carnivorous pitcher plants. They're red and have cup-like leaves.

You can expect to meet a GMC caretaker here during hiking season, near the small clearing where the AT/LT meets the pond, who will show you where to camp and who will also collect a camping fee. Because of the caretaker's presence, this place is clean. Considering the littering and abuse that could easily occur around unregulated ponds, I will gladly pay the fee.

From Stratton Pond, the LT/AT continues in a northerly direction. It follows the ravine of the Winhall River, crossing it on a bridge, and enters the Lye Brook Wilderness. Following the edge of the ravine, the trail next arrives at a junction with the Branch Pond Trail. If you need to find shelter at this point, leave the LT/AT and go south on the Branch Pond Trail one half mile to the William B. Douglas Shelter. Continuing along the LT/AT another mile further north, the LT/AT leaves the Lye Brook Wilderness and arrives at Prospect Rock. This excellent vista is located just south of the trail where it makes a sharp right turn off the dirt road (Rootville Road) it has been following. The ravine below is called Downer Glenn, the brook that made the glen is Bourn Brook, which is the brook that drains Bourn Pond. The views of Manchester and Mount Equinox from this overlook draw many day-hikers who come in from the west via Rootville Road.

The LT/AT continues, following the western rim of the mass of the Green Mountains. Below, just to the west, is the Valley of Vermont. The next stop is Spruce Peak Shelter, which is more like a cabin. It's quite large and is said to sleep sixteen. I stayed here once with my son, who was about nine at the time, along with about 25 other people, some of whom had set up tents nearby. It was a beautiful, cool, October night. Everyone there had quickly sorted out their territories and we began to talk amongst ourselves. After dark, my son and another boy his age got a fire going in the fire ring and soon most of the people there gathered around to toast marshmallows and carry on conversation.

Then someone suggested that we each tell a ghost story. As we took our turns, I could feel the energy of the group changing. Everyone was quiet, even a bit tense, and listening carefully to whomever was speaking. Then, suddenly, some crashing sounds were heard to the north. Strange lights appeared that bobbed up and down and they came closer and closer. Just when the lights were upon us and a few people were getting genuinely scared, a voice said "Is this the Spruce Peak Shelter?" It turned out that a group of six would-be hikers, carrying lanterns, axes, and large metal pots, had lost their way hours earlier. Their intrusion both interrupted and climaxed a moment of group bonding. They were lucky that a GMC caretaker wasn't on duty then to give them a good lecture about modern hiking and trip planning.

From the Spruce Peak Shelter the trail continues north, skirting the edge of the Green Mountains. A short trail to the west leads up a rock outcrop called Spruce Peak. Good views are to be had from this cute little knob (not really a peak). Another two miles or so and the LT/AT crosses Routes 30 and 11. Here, on the north side of the road, is a large hikers' parking area.

From the parking lot, which seems to be filled every summer weekend whenever the weather is good, the LT/AT begins its 2.7 mile climb of Bromley Mountain. On the way, the Bromley Tenting Area is passed, which used to be the site of a shelter. The very last section of the climb uses one of Bromley's ski trails (Runaround #1) which offers a good view of Mount Equinox. The summit of the mountain is mostly cleared, but contains two ski lift stations, the ski patrol's cabin, a few old outbuildings, and a stone pillar which serves as an LT/AT marker. Also on top is a wooden observation tower, maybe 20 feet high, that is squatter and less frightening than the towers on Glastenbury and Stratton. The views from here are excellent (see Chapter 5, page 99), especially those of Manchester, Mount Equinox, and Dorset Mountain.

The LT/AT turns left at the summit and drops into a col between Bromley's main summit and its less-traveled northern summit. This northern summit slopes down to the north very gradually, offering hikers a long walk through the boreal forest. About a half mile down, a trail on the left (west) leads to the former site of the Mad Tom Shelter which was dismantled a few years ago. Before that, it was located below in Mad Tom Notch. I'm not sure if it will be replaced, but hikers will find a modest vista to the west from this location. A further descent from Bromley's north peak leads to Mad Tom Notch and Forest Road 21 (Mad Tom Notch Road). Here is a parking area, a water pump, and a directory.

Next, the LT/AT climbs right out of Mad Tom Notch and reaches the summit of Styles Peak in 1.6 miles. (From this point to just before the Peru Peak shelter, the trail passes through the Peru Peak Wilderness.) Styles Peak is well within the boreal forest and has an eastern-facing overlook that takes in about 120 degrees of horizon. Visible from here are Magic Mountain, with its ski runs, and, in the far distance, Mount Monadnock in New Hampshire. Continuing northward, the LT/AT follows a ridgeline between peaks, climbing and descending very little for the next 1.5 miles. Almost all of this stretch is in boreal forest. Finally, the northern summit of the ridge, Peru Peak, is reached. The summit area on Peru Peak gets a good deal of use, probably from people hiking up from Griffith Lake which lies below it. There's a small lookout to the east on its wooded summit, but better views can be had by climbing a tree -- if you're very careful. Watch out, those short, stubby, and dead fir and spruce branches can hurt.

61

Baker Peak

A long descent from Peru Peak, through a woods filled with wildflowers blooming well into June and July, leads to the Peru Peak Shelter. Here, the trail leaves the Peru Peak Wilderness. This fairly large shelter, and the nearby Griffith Lake Tenting Area, are monitored during hiking season by a GMC caretaker. Fees are charged for camping. The shelter is located in a cool, dark spot, right next to a cascading brook. After a few brook crossings on mostly level terrain, the LT/AT arrives at the official tenting area on the east shore of Griffith Lake. Side trails to the west lead to the lake's shoreline.

Another quarter mile or less along the LT/AT leads to a junction with the south end of the Old Job Trail, which is really snowmobile Corridor 7 again. Just past this junction, the LT/AT enters the Big Branch Wilderness area and then meets the Lake Trail which comes up from the Valley of Vermont to the west (see Chapter 6, page 130). In just under two miles, through a relatively non-descript woods and ascending only moderately, the LT/AT suddenly meets the Baker Peak Trail, and immediately after that, Baker Peak itself.

As is described elsewhere (Chapter 5, page 119), Baker Peak is the most exposed summit-like portion of the LT/AT in the southern section of Green Mountain National Forest. It's so exposed that it even has a bypass trail to the east for bad weather hiking. The big mountain across the valley to the west is Dorset Mountain, said to be somewhat hollow now from years of marble quarrying. More distant mountains are visible under good conditions, including the Adirondacks to the west and Pico and Killington to the northeast.

The descent from Baker Peak, which is not the highest elevation of the ridge, is gradual. Two miles ahead is the Lost Pond Shelter. A more steady descent leads to a junction with the north end of the Old Job Trail, a bridge crossing of Big Branch, and the Big Branch Shelter, all within a quarter mile of each other. Another mile, mostly uphill, brings the LT/AT out to Forest Road 10.

The trail has now left the Big Branch Wilderness area. After a short road walk, you come to a paved LT/AT parking area. Opposite this, the trail again heads north into the woods which lie within the White Rocks Recreation Area. The next two miles of the trail follow brooks on fairly level ground. The Lula Tye Shelter sits uphill to the east of the LT/AT just before it meets Little Rock Pond.

63

Lula Tye was one of those hardworking women who do the necessary work that holds everything together while the men get the credit. She became corresponding secretary of the Green Mountain Club in 1926 and the next year became the treasurer. She then held both these positions for the next 29 years, precisely one orbital period of Saturn, the planet of responsibility and hard work. I stayed once at the Lula Tye shelter, sharing it with five local teenagers. When they started smoking cigarettes, my 8-year old son gave them a lecture on the vices of that habit. I didn't say a thing.

Just past the trail to the shelter is the pond. Here, facing a beautiful view of Little Rock Pond and the ledges of Green Mountain, a GMC caretaker lives during the hiking season and keeps things under control. Fees for camping apply to tent platforms, dirt tent-sites, and the two shelters near the pond. The LT/AT now follows a rocky pathway close to the eastern shore of the pond, passing a small spring along the way. At the northern end of the pond is a junction with the Green Mountain Trail (see Chapter 6, page 168), and then the Homer Stone Mountain Trail which climbs up from the valley below. After this is the Little Rock Pond Shelter which once stood on the pond's tiny island.

Over the next mile the LT/AT crosses Homer Stone Brook and then intersects an old road. In this vicinity, the trail passes through an abandoned town called Aldrichville of which virtually nothing is left. Then, it begins to climb White Rocks Mountain, passing just to the west of its true summit. Now descending, the trail passes the White Rocks Cliff Trail on the left, which drops down to a vista over the cliffs, and then the Keewaydin Trail, which descends to the White Rocks Picnic Area.

About a half mile further is the boundary of the White Rocks Recreation Area and the Greenwall Shelter. From that shelter, the LT/AT descends to Butterworth Road (with signs strongly discouraging parking here), which it follows northward and downhill to Sugar Hill Road. Another mile leads to Route 140 where limited parking is available.

This is the northern boundary of the southern section of the Green Mountain National Forest. From here the Long Trail continues northward toward Canada. Readers interested in tracing the route further north should consult the Green Mountain Club's *Long Trail Guide*.

Joining the Green Mountain Club

The Green Mountain Club is the group to join if you are interested in hiking in southern Vermont. Hikers need to unite, to become part of a group that will lobby for them when situations arise that affect the land and trails. Consider the greater lobbying power the snowmobilers have with their 35,000-member Vermont Association of Snow Travelers, compared to only 8,000 members of the Green Mountain Club. Perhaps the main reason why there are fewer hiking members is because hikers, have not been required to obtain permits and pay fees to practice their sport as the snowmobilers do. I urge all who hike the Green Mountains to join this group, if only to keep in touch with developments in land use and conditions along the Long Trail.

The Green Mountain Club publishes the invaluable *Long Trail Guide* which details the route of the trail throughout the state of Vermont and includes maps. They also publish a set of maps of the entire Long Trail (End-to-End) and several other publications that are of interest to hikers. Members receive the quarterly publication *Long Trail News* and pay discounted fees at high use shelters and camping areas. You can contact the club at the address and numbers below.

Green Mountain Club, Inc.

> 4711 Waterbury-Stowe Road
> Waterbury Center, VT 05677
> Phone: 802/244-7037 Fax: 802/244-5867
> e-mail: gmc@sover.net
> *www.greenmountainclub.org*

Chapter 4

The Wilderness Areas

The four wilderness areas of the southern section of the Green Mountain National Forest offer exceptional opportunities for experienced hikers and backpackers who value wildness. These areas are not for everyone, however. Hikers who expect groomed trails and designated hiking areas should go elsewhere; wilderness areas offer only a few trails, some of them degenerated old logging roads that barely penetrate the forest. Anyone entering these wilderness areas should be in good shape, familiar with map and compass, and prepared for problems. The rewards that the experience offers are subtle but ultimately profound.

Wilderness areas exist not for the practical needs of humans, but for our spiritual needs. Interested readers who wish to explore this idea in some depth should check out Roderick Frazier Nash's book *Wilderness and the American Mind*, and also Laura and Guy Waterman's excellent book *Wilderness Ethics*.

On September 3, 1964, Congress passed the Wilderness Act and designated specific tracts of land to be set aside as wilderness. The Act defines wilderness as areas affected primarily by nature, not by humans -- places where nature is to be left to its own devices and humans are merely visitors. Wilderness areas are designated by Congress and then protected and managed in such a way that the natural ecological processes operate on their own terms. They are undeveloped, federally-owned parcels of land, generally over 5,000 acres, where humans may not establish a permanent presence. Motorized vehicles are not permitted in wilderness areas, though hunting is allowed according to state regulations.

Unlike the more open wilderness areas of the American west, southern Vermont's wilderness areas are very difficult to penetrate due to the thick, unrestricted growth of forest. Don't let the relatively small size of these wilderness areas lead you to underestimate them. Passage through one of these areas can be very challenging, and doing so requires a great deal of patience and respect for nature. Because of these difficulties, the wilderness areas are only lightly used. Summer travel is particularly demanding due to thick growth and bugs, while winter travel, on snowshoes or cross-country skis, is often easier. Solo travel is not recommended.

The George D. Aiken Wilderness

South of Route 9 is the 5,060 acre George D. Aiken Wilderness, a high plateau of forest and wetlands. Because it is nearly trailless, few enter the area. Those that do will find travel quite challenging as the wilderness is punctuated with both new and abandoned beaver ponds. Where a map may show a pond, the hiker may find only a meadow, and ponds may be found where none are shown on the map. Anyone who enters this wilderness should be ready for some challenging orienteering, mud, encounters with wildlife (including bear and moose), and long stretches of dense woodland with few useful landmarks. The Forest Service offers a free map of the area which can supplement the USGS provisional topographic maps (Stamford and Woodford quads).

This wilderness area is named for a leading advocate of wilderness protection, Vermont Senator George D. Aiken (1892-1984). Aiken was a farmer who held a succession of public offices, first in Vermont and later in the U.S. Senate. In the 1930s he was elected governor of Vermont. During the same period he also wrote two books, *Pioneering with Wildflowers* and *Pioneering with Fruits and Berries*. He entered the U.S. Senate in 1940 and remained there, re-elected every six years, until 1974.

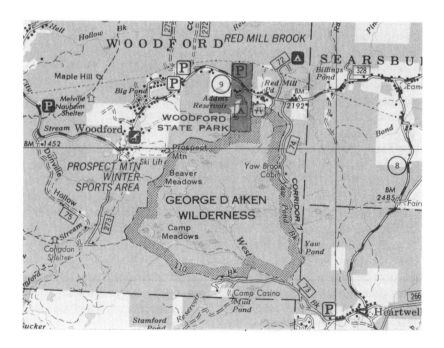

In the Senate, Aiken won a reputation for integrity and independence, often crossing the aisle from his fellow Republicans and voting for Democratic causes. He fought Senator Joseph McCarthy during the 1950s and criticized the American involvement in Viet Nam in the 1960s. Aiken was also the first to propose the food stamp program for low-income families. Beginning in the early 1970s, Aiken fought to bring the National Wilderness Preservation System to Vermont and other eastern states. His efforts led to legislation that made possible the wilderness that now goes by his name, as well as others in the east. The George D. Aiken Wilderness was designated by Congress in 1984.

As mentioned, the terrain of the Aiken Wilderness is high, over 2,300 feet in elevation. There are no steep drops or mountains in the area, which means that water drainage through it is slow. The area is definitely wet -- bogs and marshes are everywhere. An abundance of water, especially standing water, generally guarantees a high population of biting flies, a condition that may require some serious insect repellent.

Trailheads

There are several ways to enter the George D. Aiken Wilderness. From Route 9, at a point 9.4 miles west of Wilmington and 12.2 miles east of Bennington, Forest Road 74 turns south and ends at a clearing. A very primitive extension of the road continues southward, essentially marking the eastern boundary of the wilderness area. This clearing, suitable for parking, is 1.6 miles south of Route 9. Along the way are turnouts often occupied by "dispersed" campers practicing a kind of car-camping. This area is extremely active during the winter, with the Forest Road being a major snowmobile corridor.

Another approach is just west of Routes 8 and 100, 0.7 miles south of their junction in Heartwellville. After crossing a small bridge over the West Branch of the Deerfield River, you should find a snowmobile trailhead parking area on the left and Forest Road 73 heading into the forest. While you can park at this trailhead parking area and walk in, there is also room for several cars closer to the Aiken Wilderness ahead of you. Drive one mile west from the trailhead parking, going up a rise and then down it. Park just before you come to a bridge over the river. The lane to your right (north) that heads down to the confluence of Yaw Pond Brook and the West Branch of the Deerfield River is a way into this wilderness. Forest Road 73, a rough, gravel road, is safe for most cars, though I wouldn't drive too fast. My Toyota has successfully navigated it.

A third access point is via Woodford State Park, located south of Route 9 10.3 miles west of Wilmington and 11.3 miles east of Bennington. This park offers car camping and family recreation, and its focal point is the Adams Reservoir, a scenic body of water that was created during the 19th century when its waters were used to power sawmills. Parts of the reservoir are quite wild. Standing dead trees on the south end contrast with the beaches of the day-use area. A loop trail encircles the reservoir and at its southernmost point, the trail actually enters the Aiken Wilderness.

Finally, the Prospect Mountain Ski Area trail system also penetrates the Aiken Wilderness. This cross-country ski area is open during the summer (for a fee) to mountain bikes and hiking. The Mountain Trail winds up and around the mountain, formerly a downhill ski area, and just grazes the wilderness area. During winter, experienced leaders take groups on ski tours out to the wilderness. Because the area is so wet, cross-country skiing is an excellent alternative way to explore it. Snowmobiles and other motorized vehicles are not permitted in the wilderness.

Exploring the George D. Aiken Wilderness

The Yaw Pond Trail

On several occasions I've attempted to enter the Aiken Wilderness. Each time I was beset with challenges, but also presented with amazing sights and a true sense of remoteness. Unlike the Lye Brook Wilderness which is near Manchester airport, the Aiken Wilderness seems to be located in a zone that even planes avoid.

An easy way to experience the edge of the Aiken Wilderness is on the Yaw Pond Trail, which is actually an old railroad bed and skid road. In winter it's a snowmobile corridor that links Route 9 with Heartwellville. To hike it, drive in from Heartwellville on Forest Road 73 and park just before the bridge over the river. You could also walk FR 73 from the trailhead parking, if you prefer. On the right side of the road, find the lane that leads down toward the river. Walk a very short distance and turn right (north) onto the Yaw Pond Trail (unmarked and unmaintained) at a briar patch. After a few yards of pushing through bushes, the trail begins to look more like a trail. A short distance ahead you may find yourself blocked by a beaver pond that has recently flooded the trail. The dam is just to your left. This kind of thing is typical of the area. Still, it is nature in full gear, something you don't see in many other places.

Perhaps you will visit the area when the beavers have moved on and their dam has broken. If so, just keep following the pathway. If the trail is flooded, sidehill (that's scoot up the slope) on your right and then cross over the north end of the beaver pond. At this point you should be at edge of Yaw Pond Brook. Follow the trail alongside the brook on a rocky wet path where you may find clusters of honey fungus mushrooms growing in late summer. Soon you will come to a bridge of sorts, that spans Yaw Pond Brook. Just before the crossing, a snowmobile trail continues to the northeast. Cross this bridge at your own risk; it's made of some old steel supports covered with snow fence.

After crossing, the trail turns right and continues its northward journey into the Yaw Pond area. It was flooded the last time I was there and tends to be very wet even during dry periods. I've never been able to get any farther then this. But I did see many frogs and would recommend this route for a nature walk, if not a real hike.

In Quest of Camp Meadows

Please note that this excursion is suggested only for serious explorers of trailless areas who know how to use a topographic map, a compass, and common sense. Solo travel is not recommended. The one trail (or more accurately, the dotted line on the topo map) that penetrates the George D. Aiken Wilderness starts just before the bridge over the Deerfield on Forest Road 73. After crossing Yaw Pond Brook, it follows alongside the Deerfield River, then leaves it to follow Camp Meadows Brook, and finally terminates at a "building" in the middle of nowhere.

One fine summer day I parked my car at the bridge and crossed Yaw Pond Brook on the remnants of an old, disintegrating bridge, which, as you read this, may no longer exist. A crossing of the brook on rocks is still possible, however, under normal conditions. After passing a beautiful little meadow and pond on the right, the trail heads west following an old, rocky railbed. Not much farther along, the trail dwindles into a barely discernible footpath. Keep left and close to river here and you should arrive at a campsite.

The "trail" continues west, still following the north side of the river, passing through many wet areas, until it finally meets a second and smaller campsite at the edge of the river. It took me about a half hour of walking to reach this site. Technically, both campsites on this trail are illegal because they are too close to the water's edge.

On the way to Camp Meadows

The second camp is located at a rocky confluence of waters. The trail itself seems to disappear into the brook. I crossed the brook here, staying with my westerly course, and tried to find a continuation of the trail ahead, which the map said was there. All I found were sections of trail and I spent most of the time fighting through overgrown meadows and crossing small brooks, then eventually a larger brook flowing east. This I identified as Camp Meadows Brook.

If you can find this larger brook, cross it where rocks make it possible, and stay on its north side heading west. There is a fairly obvious trail here that gradually rises above the brook. It's much easier to follow than the previous section and leads in about a mile to the eastern edge of Camp Meadows. The map shows a pond, but only a wet meadow remains. Near what was once the pond is a broken down cabin, its metal roof preserving the rotting wood under it. Two free-standing woodstoves guard the building from outside of it.

71

The last section of the trail that leads to the cabin and pond requires some serious punching through a barrier of thick fir trees interspersed with wet areas. To make matters worse, there's also an abundance of prickly bushes. It took me an hour to find this area from the brook crossing at the second campsite. From here, however, the hiker seeking solitude could continue north on a low ridge between wet areas, make camp, and possibly see no one for weeks, and probably months. In truth, the area was overwhelmingly wild and I felt that I had entered a kind of lost world. The view over the nearby meadow, from the old beaver dam, conveyed a wildness similar to some of the Western deserts I've camped in.

My return trip from Camp Meadows was quite exciting. I was able to get back to roughly the point where I crossed Camp Meadows Brook with no problem. There, on the top of a flat rock near the edge of the brook, were a number of unidentifiable metal parts laid out as if they were part of an unlabeled museum display. Someone had collected them and then left them exposed.

I crossed the brook and headed east, but couldn't find signs of my previous route coming in. Entering a large wet area interspersed with hummocks of tall grasses and tiny areas of forest, I noticed that, in places, the grasses were pressed down, as if some large animal had slept there. Unable to recognize any features I had passed on the way in, I became concerned about my location -- Where was I? To go forward or to my left was impossible, the ground was too wet. I consulted my compass to reassure myself that I wasn't lost in the larger sense, just only in the smaller sense. Then, looking down to the ground I noticed that I was standing right next to a substantial pile of moose pellets, and they were steaming.

The rustling of bushes to my right drew my attention and I found myself looking directly into the eyes of a large moose, the size of a horse. I froze for a moment. The moose moved a few yards to the west. I thought about taking a picture, decided not to push my luck, and then slowly worked my way around her, keeping as far as I could from her but staying out of the mud. The direction I chose was south. My plan was to get out of this old meadow as quickly as possible and head for higher ground. With my map and compass I did so and found Reservoir Brook and crossed it. Beyond the brook was Forest Road 73. An easy mile down the road took me back to my car.

Such are the experiences, exhilarating and exhausting, one can have in the George D. Aiken Wilderness.

The Lye Brook Wilderness

In January of 1975 the Lye Brook Wilderness was one of the first two wilderness areas designated in Vermont. It is the largest wilderness area in the southern section of Green Mountain National Forest and is located just to the east of Manchester, the most touristy of tourist towns in the region. It embraces a 15,680 acre tract of high plateau just east of Route 7 and Manchester that was heavily logged during the early 20th century. Unlike the trailless George D. Aiken wilderness, there are two trails plus a short section of the Appalachian Trail which allow visitors to enter it without great difficulty.

One of the trails that penetrates the Lye Brook Wilderness is the Lye Brook Trail. After a gradual climb out of Lye Brook Hollow, this former railroad bed attains the high plateau and comes to Bourn Pond. It then continues westward to Stratton Pond. The second trail is the north-south trending Branch Pond Trail, which extends from Arlington-West Wardsboro Road and passes both Branch Pond and Bourn Pond before reaching the Long Trail/Appalachian Trail. Portions of the Branch Pond Trail also follow old railroad beds. Years ago, the LT/AT ran from Stratton Pond, which is about two miles due east, around Bourn Pond and then north to Prospect Rock. Today, the LT/AT is routed away from Bourn Pond, and the Branch Pond Trail utilizes the old LT/AT path northward.

Four USGS topographic maps cover the area: Manchester, Sunderland, Londonderry, and Stratton. The Forest Service provisional editions show the wilderness boundaries.

The western edge of the Lye Brook Wilderness, known locally as East Mountain, is quite visible to those in the Manchester-Arlington valley. Route 7 runs parallel and below this steep and abrupt wall of forest that reveals the fault line between the Green Mountains and the Taconic Range with extreme clarity. From the highway or the valley between the two ranges, East Mountain appears at first glance to be featureless, but a second look will reveal a few openings through which flow streams.

The Lye Brook Wilderness is named for one of these streams, Lye Brook, which cuts through the middle of its area. It has carved out, over millions of years, Lye Brook Hollow, which is quite visible from Route 7 heading south towards Manchester. The southern boundary of the wilderness is marked by the Mill Brook gorge. The northern boundary is marked by Downer Glen, known for Prospect Rock, and through which Bourn Brook flows.

73

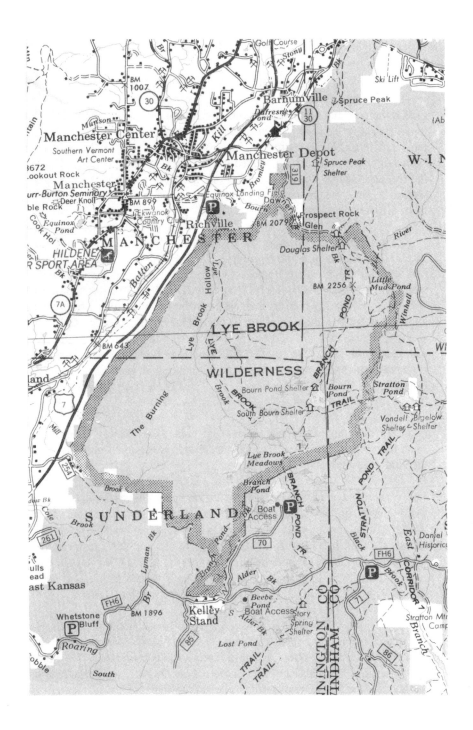

CONTOUR INTERVAL 20 FEET

The Lye Brook Wilderness was once the scene of a major lumbering operation. In 1914 the Rich Lumber Company set up shop near the base of Lye Brook Hollow, brought in workers, including a large number of Italian and Swedish laborers, and proceeded to remove as much balsam and spruce as they could from the high plateau above Manchester. A railroad line was built that took cars up the mountain via Lye Brook Hollow, and out to the broad and mostly flat high area to the east. The Rich Lumber Company's base of operations at the foot of the high plateau, which included their sawmill, became a company town called Richville. In only five years they managed to clear-cut a tract of land they thought would take 15 years to ravage. Then a fire took out their sawmill. The game was up, the workers were laid off, and the company left town.

The Lye Brook Trail

Hikers will find a good-sized circular parking area at the trailhead for the Lye Brook Trail, along with a directory that gives distances to various destinations. The trailhead, which is labeled Entry Point 4 on the Forest Service "Wilderness Times" map, is just east of Manchester. From the point where Route 7 passes over the Routes 11 & 30 intersection, drive east on Routes 11 & 30 for about 0.5 mile and turn right (south) onto East Manchester Road. Follow this road, which will swing to the west, for just over one mile. Turn left onto Glenn Road, and in 0.1 mile keep to the right. You are now on Lye Brook Road, a gravel road (watch for the bump). The trailhead is less than 0.5 mile ahead.

An alternate approach is from Manchester Center, heading east on Routes 11 & 30. Turn right onto Richardville Road, then in 0.5 mile, left onto East Manchester Road. A right turn onto Glenn Road, which leads to Lye Brook Road, is 0.7 mile ahead.

The Lye Brook Trail is blazed occasionally with blue markers. From the trailhead, the Lye Brook Trail enters the woods, comes to a small clearing, and turns left just before the railroad grade that runs alongside the brook. This portion of the Lye Brook Trail parallels the former rail line that penetrated the wilderness. Because parts of the original track bed have been washed away by erosion, the trail does not use its route and begins climbing the north wall of Lye Brook Hollow on wood roads. About a mile into the hike is an area of downed trees, apparently blown down by intense local winds in 1995.

Most hikers entering the Lye Brook Wilderness from the Manchester trailhead seek the great waterfalls that cascade down to Lye Brook. These are found at a junction 1.8 miles into the hike. To reach them, turn right onto a grade that slopes downhill. After about 0.5 mile you'll find the falls, really a series of cascades, on your left pouring down from high above through a sharp and narrow crack in the wall of the hollow. Be careful on these ledges. These unnamed falls are said to be the highest in Vermont.

If you make it to the falls, consider this. The old logging railroad grade entered Lye Brook Hollow near the trailhead and followed Lye Brook for about two miles. Just south of the falls, the line ended. Here, the train would move ahead on extra track, a rail switch would be thrown, and the train would back up to the next level. That switchback is the rail bed you turned onto to reach the falls. Then, at the junction with the Lye Brook Trail proper, the engine would move forward again, switched onto tracks leading up to the plateau. From there it extended deeper into the forest, crossing over a high trestle at one point. Along the way to Bourn Pond were several lumber camps, one near Lye Brook Meadows.

You can find remnants of the old rail line in the vicinity of the falls. On the opposite bank, over the "cave," the switchback continues and passes another set of falls. Below the falls and downstream near Lye Brook, are some stone ruins that were once used for storing dynamite used to blast out the route of the railroad. These ruins are not easy to find or get to, and the climb back up is difficult. Those familiar with the arts of forest navigation might try following the old railroad bed alongside Lye Brook all the way back to the trailhead. Much of it has been washed away, necessitating some scrambling along steep banks, slogging through wet areas, or boulder-hopping in the brook.

The hike to the falls and back is certainly one of the classic Green Mountain National Forest day hikes and is highly recommended. After a stop at the falls, most hikers will have had enough and will head back the way they came to the trailhead. Those that follow the Lye Brook Trail beyond the turnoff to the falls should be prepared for a long walk to Bourn Pond on a less-used trail. For the next 5.3 miles the trail, after leveling off, traverses wetlands, beaver ponds, and meadows. It passes close to a remote section of the wilderness called Lye Brook Meadows and then arrives at the southern end of Bourn Pond where a shelter is located. The last two miles of the trail, which passes some old clearings, offers much solitude. In contrast, summer weekends at Bourn Pond can often be crowded. The Lye Brook Trail continues eastward from Bourn Pond, crosses the wilderness boundary and, after 1.9 miles, meets the LT/AT at Stratton Pond. The full length, from the Manchester trailhead to Stratton Pond, is 9.2 miles.

The Branch Pond Trail *[See Map #2, Chapter 7, pages 158-159]*

This 8.3 mile-long trail begins on Arlington-West Wardsboro Road and travels north to a junction with the LT/AT, far from any road. The southern trailhead is not very distinct, and there's parking for only one car on the north side of the road. Just ahead of this spot, near an overlook, is room for another car. The trailhead is located 9.3 miles west of Route 100 (1.2 miles west of the parking area for the Stratton Pond Trail) and 8.5 miles east of North Road, which leads to East Arlington.

The southern section of the Branch Pond Trail, between Arlington-West Wardsboro Road and Bourn Pond, travels through some relatively high woodland at elevations between 2,600 and 3,000 ft. The northern section, from Bourn Pond to its junction with the Appalachian Trail, is lower, at one point descending to about 2,200 feet. At the higher elevations, hikers will pass through areas that are almost boreal in vegetation. Spruce, fir, ferns, and clintonia will make it seem as if you're near a ridgeline. The views through the forest, however, will confirm that you are really in a high and remote world of ponds and meadows -- the land of the beaver.

From its southern trailhead the Branch Pond trail heads uphill and north, descends and then climbs again to just under 3,000 feet in elevation. Here the trail skirts the eastern side of an unnamed hill of about 3,080 feet in elevation. A long descent leads to a trail junction. From here, a trail heads west for 0.3 miles to the Branch Pond parking area at the end of Forest Road 70. This connection point, 1.8 miles from the trailhead, is labeled Entry Point 5 on the Forest Service "Wilderness Times" map of the Lye Brook Wilderness. Continuing north on the Branch Pond Trail, a few small streams will be crossed before arriving at a junction with a path that heads west and downhill to Branch Pond. Since Branch Pond is just a short walk from the parking area off Forest Road 70, there are usually people nearby, many of them with canoes. The path down to the pond is only about 0.1 mile and leads to a few very small openings onto the water.

After passing the path to the pond, the Branch Pond Trail enters the Lye Brook Wilderness. From here to Bourn Pond the route traverses a few small rises and, at a recent relocation, skirts a meadow by climbing a small hill. Next, a section of an old railroad bed becomes the trail's pathway, and at 4.3 miles a junction with the Lye Brook Trail is reached. Just to the left is the South Bourn Shelter, which lies in the midst of a spider-web of paths. The Lye Brook Trail heads west behind the shelter, the Branch Pond Trail swings around the west shore of the pond in front of and below the shelter. Along the west shore of the pond, north of the shelter, are a few tent-sites, and a little further still is a trail to the Bourn Pond North Shore Tenting Area.

79

From Bourn Pond, the Branch Pond Trail continues north on the railroad bed, crosses Bourn Brook and, further on, follows near to it. This is the same railroad from Lye Brook Hollow, portions of which are utilized by the Lye Brook and Branch Pond Trails. (Although the Branch Pond Trail departs from it, some readers may want to know that the original line continued north, then turned east and south, almost reaching Stratton Pond.) At 7.8 miles from the trailhead, the trail passes the William B. Douglass shelter, and 0.5 miles further, reaches its terminus at the Long Trail/Appalachian Trail. This final junction, Entry Point 3 according to the Forest Service, is located on the boundary of the wilderness area.

From its junction with the Branch Pond Trail, the LT/AT skirts the boundary of the Lye Brook Wilderness at the edge of Downer Glenn for just under a mile. Its route here follows Rootville Road, a dirt road coming up from Manchester Depot. At the point where the LT/AT turns away from the Wilderness is one of Manchester's premier hiking destinations, Prospect Rock.

Prospect Rock

Prospect Rock is a popular day-hike's lookout that offers excellent views out over Manchester and Mount Equinox. It is included in this section of the guidebook because it is only a few yards from the Lye Brook Wilderness boundary. To reach the trailhead from Routes 11 & 30, about a half mile east of the Route 7 overpass in Manchester, turn south onto East Manchester Road. Make an immediate left (east) onto Rootville Road and drive 0.6 miles to the end of the main road. Park near the water tank, but don't block driveways or park where there are "no parking" signs. High clearance vehicles may be able to go a little farther to a small parking area in the woods past the last house on the road.

The walk to Prospect Rock follows old Rootville Road for 1.5 miles, all uphill with a 1,100 foot elevation gain. Along the way you'll pass a dark hemlock ravine, a few streams, and some views over Downer Glenn through birch trees. Prospect Rock will be on your right, where Rootville Road meets the LT/AT. Opposite Prospect Rock, the LT/AT turns north into the woods.

One crisp fall day my son and I hiked to Prospect Rock along Rootville Road. On the way back we encountered a man driving an all-terrain-vehicle (ATV) who was clearing dead branches off the road. Five minutes later a high clearance truck passed us that was loaded with vacuum cleaners and guns. My son was very impressed with the guns and his interest in our hike increased dramatically.

I had a different reaction. Four or five more vehicles, SUVs and pickups, passed us as we descended, most with similar cargo. I spoke with one of the drivers who told me they were headed for their hunting camp to get it ready for hunting season. The USGS topographic map shows a small parcel of private land and a building just off Rootville Road, which I must assume is where they were headed. One map shows it to be the Sweezey Camp. It's very close to the LT/AT and not too far from the Douglass Shelter. I relate this story so that hikers will stay alert and won't forget that hunting is allowed in the wilderness areas.

Other Features of the Lye Brook Wilderness

The Forest Service map entitled "The Wilderness Times Featuring Lye Brook" draws attention to several areas that may be of interest to bushwhackers. The waterfalls and railroad beds have already been described. Another feature worth bushwhacking to is the quartzite rock fields, high on the western rim of Lye Brook Hollow. These are past the falls, well above the Lye Brook on hill 2619. You can see these from Route 7 just north of Manchester and also from Routes 11 and 30. Reaching these wild rocks requires following Lye Brook for over a mile past the falls and then bushwhacking up the steep-sided gorge. Only experienced land navigators in top condition should attempt this hike.

Also further south of the falls, on the other side of Lye Brook and on the top of the plateau, is an area called "The Burning." Early in the 20th century, a lightning fire burned up many acres which then became a favorite berry picking area. Looking down on the area from Mount Equinox, "The Burning" is an elongated stretch of evergreens that extend from the ledges over Lye Brook, then south and west for about two miles. The Lye Brook Meadows, to the south of the Lye Brook Trail before it reaches Bourn Pond, is a wild area where beavers have created a number of ponds and meadows. Some charcoal kilns are to be found in the woods just to the east of the Branch Pond Trail and south of the LT/AT uphill from the Douglas Shelter. All of the above areas are hard to reach. Only those with a good map, a compass, and good woods sense will find them.

The Big Branch and Peru Peak Wilderness

North of Mad Tom Notch and Forest Road 21, and south of Forest Road 10 are two side-by-side wilderness areas. They are both components of the 36,400 acre White Rocks National Recreation Area that was designated on June 19, 1984. A national recreation area is a multi-purpose management area which may include sections designated as wilderness.

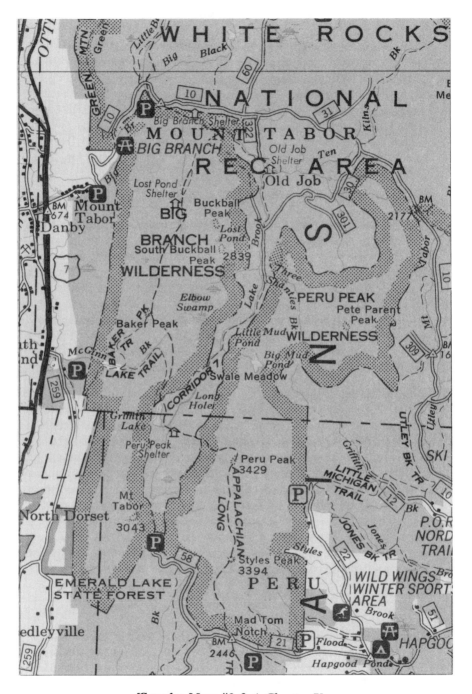

[See also Maps #3 & 4, Chapter 7]

82

Both the Big Branch and Peru Peak wilderness areas appear on the Forest Service's map, "National Recreation Area Times Featuring White Rocks." Both are also completely covered by the USGS Danby quadrangle. Note: There are two Danby quadrangles. The standard USGS 7-1/2-minute quad shows the territory. The Provisional edition quad (available from the Forest Service) shows the Wilderness boundaries as well as the information contained on the standard quad.

What's obvious to anyone looking at a map of these two wilderness areas is that they are adjacent to each other. The main reason they are not one unified area is that between them lies a major snowmobile corridor, and motorized vehicles are not allowed within wilderness areas. As has already been mentioned elsewhere, snowmobiles have a major presence in Green Mountain National Forest, and their corridor would have been blocked by a single wilderness area. Running through the narrow gap between the Big Branch Wilderness on the west and the Peru Peak Wilderness on the east is Corridor 7, the north-south snowmobile superhighway.

There are several natural features encompassed by these two wilderness areas that are of interest to hikers. Lake Brook and Big Branch are two wild and scenic streams that drain the area. While only 2,834 feet in elevation, Baker Peak has a small exposed ridgeline. Griffith Lake, which sits between the two wilderness areas, is a remote pond that was once the site of a hotel. Today, there is a designated camping area right next to it, and a trail shelter a half mile away, both monitored by the Green Mountain Club. A trail system in the area offers circuit hike possibilities. One loop hike, described in Chapter 7, page 165, utilizes the LT/AT and the Old Job Trail. The Old Job Trail passes through the site of an old lumber camp where the remains of former human habitation are trailside scenery, including a monster sawdust pile and a scraggly, abandoned apple orchard.

The Big Branch Wilderness is named for the Big Branch brook which crashes down one of the few breaks in the long wall of the Green Mountains just east of Route 7. A large portion of both Big Branch and Peru Peak Wilderness areas drains into Big Branch which then empties into Otter Creek in Danby, which itself flows north to empty into Lake Champlain. The Forest Service maintains a scenic picnic ground on the edge of the Big Branch gorge which is located on Forest Road 10 (Danby-Landgrove Road), 2.6 miles east of Route 7 in Danby. Besides the drop-off into the gorge, there's a good view of Dorset Mountain from the picnic area. Also found here is one of two trailheads for the Green Mountain Trail, which leads to Little Rock Pond and may be used as part of a loop hike. (See Chapter 7, page 168.)

Beaver lodge in the Big Branch Wilderness

At the heart of the Big Branch Wilderness is Baker Peak, the rockiest summit-like exposure in the southern section of Green Mountain National Forest. 100 yards or more of bare rock with a great view of Dorset Mountain makes Baker Peak a popular destination for hikers. The truth is that Baker Peak is not the actual summit of the ridge, but it sure seems to be if one approaches the peak from the south. The most dramatic approach is from Danby via the Lake Trail and then the Baker Peak Trail. For more information on Baker Peak, see Chapter 5, page 119.

The Peru Peak Wilderness is named for one of the higher peaks of the area. Its sister peak, Styles Peak, is just south of it, and the two are connected by a ridgeline trail that traverses a boreal forest. The LT/AT climbs steeply from Mad Tom Notch, at the southern boundary of the wilderness, for 1.6 miles to Styles Peak, where there is a vista out to the east and south. In another 1.7 miles the summit of Peru Peak is reached, which offers a similar, though somewhat more modest vista.

While the strenuous, nearly 1,000-foot climb from Mad Tom Notch to the summit of Style Peak is no joke, the walk between the two sister peaks can be a stroll through another world. Along with the spruce, fir, clintonia, and other plant species of the boreal forest, there are many little birds. If you come to an area where a group of birds have congregated, stop and keep still for a moment. By making a psssh-psssh kind of sound by blowing air through your lips, you may stimulate the curiosity of a few of the many warblers that inhabit or visit this high forest. The climb up Styles Peak and the northern descent off Peru Peak on the LT/AT are also great places to find spring wildflowers.

The northern section of the Peru Peak Wilderness is trailless. Just off the Old Job Trail (Corridor 7) north of Griffith Lake are Little and Big Mud Pond. Little Mud Pond can be found by following an old woods road which meets the Old Job Trail just north of the bridge over the pond's drainage into Lake Brook. First, climb over an embankment (presumably built to keep snowmobiles out of the wilderness area), then follow the path to a fork, keep right and follow the stream past a waterfall (spectacular in spring), and up to the shore of the pond. This is a remote and very wild place. I once spoke with another hiker who had just spotted several moose near Little Mud Pond. Indeed, moose hoofprints are common in this vicinity along the muddy Old Job Trail.

Northeast of the two mud ponds is a rocky ridge that extends northward to Forest Road 10 and beyond. The high point here is Pete Parent Peak which reaches 2,962 feet in elevation. This ridge drops somewhat, but not too much, to the high pass on Forest Road 10 at Devil's Den. There are some limited views of the Peru Peak Wilderness from this area and also farther west on FR 10. Forest Road 30, which turns south of FR 10 about 1.5 miles west of Devil's Den, is another way to access the wilderness. Trailhead parking is found at the terminus of FR 30, 2.3 miles south of FR 10. This area is next to Lake Brook and the Old Job Trail. You can expect to find "dispersed" car campers here during summer.

I once attempted to reach Pete Parent Peak from the Old Job Trail. One beautiful spring day, my son, his friend, and I walked up the gravel road that turns off the Old Job Trail and ends at the Peru Peak Wilderness boundary. My plan was to follow a trail indicated on the map to a point about a mile due west of the peak, then bushwack to the summit. We were prepared, as anyone should be who enters a wilderness area, with several maps, a compass, and other supplies.

Within a few minutes of walking, the trail that was indicated on the map became impassable. Next, we were suddenly accosted by swarms of blackflies, mosquitoes, and several other types of flying insects I didn't recognize. They completely ignored our citronella-based repellent so I broke out my container of 100% Deet, which is for emergency use only. It had absolutely no effect on them. They entered our noses and ears and we even swallowed a few.

As we went deeper into the forest I became concerned about the maps -- they didn't correlate with reality. The USGS Provisional map, Danby quad (available from the Forest Service), shows a trail on the south side of Three Shanties Brook, which is the one I had hoped to find as it would bring us close to the peak. What we found were several parallel old logging roads, almost completely overgrown and impossible to follow in places. They were muddy, too. Another map I had with me was an earlier 15-minute Wallingford quadrangle which shows a trail on the north side of the brook. As far as I could tell, this trail wasn't there at all. After considerable bushwhacking, we managed to reach a point near the end of the brook, as it is shown on the map. We might have continued our punishing journey, but all three of us were nearing our physical and mental limits and I decided to call it quits. Such is bushwhacking in a Green Mountain wilderness area, a place "where man himself is a visitor who does not remain." No kidding.

Readers should not get the idea that I'm trying to discourage hiking into any of the four wilderness areas described above. On the contrary, I recommend it -- with proper preparation and proper attitude, of course. In the wilderness, a defeat may be more important to us arrogant humans than a conquest.

Chapter 5

Hiking the Mountains

The Summits over 1,000 Meters

There are eight summits over 1,000 meters (3,280 feet) in the southern section of the Green Mountain National Forest, and two or possibly three of them are unnamed. There are two additional peaks over 1,000 meters that are within the overall boundaries of the Forest, though not under Forest Service management. These are the Taconic peaks, Equinox and Dorset, which are respectively the second and third highest in southern Vermont. The 1,000 meter mark is approximately the elevation that the boreal forest, mostly fir and spruce, begins in southern Vermont. None of the summits in this region extend into an alpine zone. Still, most offer a good climb, some vistas, and the cool, moist experience of the evergreen northern forest. A peakbagger's list of these summits follows this section.

Haystack Mountain: 1,052 m, 3445 ft.

To my eyes, Haystack is the most perfectly formed peak in the southern Green Mountains. In the fall its sharp green cone tops off a broad expanse of color, while in winter the summit evergreens hold the frost, giving the peak a stunning white topping. My favorite views of Haystack are from the White House on Route 9 just east of Wilmington, and heading east and downhill on Route 9 past Searsburg. Another great view of it is from the southern end of the Harriman Reservoir. The major ski area that is located on its eastern flanks is barely noticeable. Even from its summit peak, the scars of the ski industry are minor, something that can't be said for its neighbor, Mount Snow. Haystack also stands tall above the encroaching hominid hives below (a large residential development sprawls along its southeastern flanks). The winding roads of this development must be negotiated before Haystack can be climbed, but again, this is barely noticeable from afar or from the summit itself. Amazing!

I've climbed Haystack in all seasons and continue to find it an enjoyable and relatively easy hike. The elevation gain is about 1,045 feet or 318 meters, enough for a mild workout, but not too difficult for children. In winter, however, you can expect to encounter snowmobiles on the way up, though not at the very summit which is attained by a footpath.

The Haystack Ski Area, part of the Mount Snow Resort, utilizes a portion of the eastern face of the mountain, but not near the summit. The true summit can be seen only briefly from two of the ski lifts. An excellent view of Haystack Pond, however, is to be found from a cliff at the top of the ski area, just off what is called the Deerfield Ridge Trail. Haystack Pond used to be called Sylvan Lake. Some believe it occupies a hollow called a cirque, that was scooped out by an ancient mountain glacier.

To find the trailhead to Haystack, drive 1.1 miles west on Route 9 from the traffic lights in Wilmington and turn right (north) into the Chimney Hill development on Haystack Road. After going 1.2 miles, turn left at a staggered four-way junction onto Chimney Hill Road. Make the next right onto Binney Brook Road and follow the steep and winding dirt road to an intersection with Upper Dam Road. Turn right here and, keeping to the main road, drive another 0.6 mile to the trailhead that is located on the right at a turn in the road. There is parking for a few cars alongside the road. The elevation here is about 2,400 feet or 732 meters.

The moderate climb to the summit will take 1.5-to-2 hours. The distance to the summit is said to be 2.4 miles, though it seems shorter to me. From the trailhead, follow the Haystack Trail uphill. The trail begins as a gravel road, passes a gate and then levels off. After about 10 minutes of walking, turn left onto a footpath marked with blue plastic tags. A sign here indicates that you are on the Haystack Trail. The trail, now a well-worn dirt and rock footpath, descends and rises twice before it swings around to the right and gradually climbs to a shoulder of the mountain. Along the path you may notice the glistening mica schist in the bedrock. At the shoulder you will enter a clearing where part of the mountain's summit is visible to your right. In this area the smell of balsam fir fills the air and the woods begin to take on a northern appearance with white birch and black spruce the prominent species. The trail, now more of a woods road (called Deerfield Ridge Trail on maps) is level for a short distance here.

Be alert for the next turn. After passing a rock outcrop on your left, look for a trail coming in on the right. It's located about 100 yards past the rock outcrop and (in 1998) was marked with an old wooden "Haystack Mountain" sign. Turn right onto this trail and begin the final path to the summit. Blue tags will appear occasionally on your way up. The steep, needle-covered and fern-lined trail is stunning in its wild beauty. Here you will find many of the plants of the northern forest, a very different plant community than you passed through on the way up. A small footpath goes off to the right -- ignore it. In about 15 minutes or less, you will reach the summit. Walk straight ahead over the large rock outcropping and you'll find an excellent clearing that overlooks Haystack Pond and points beyond.

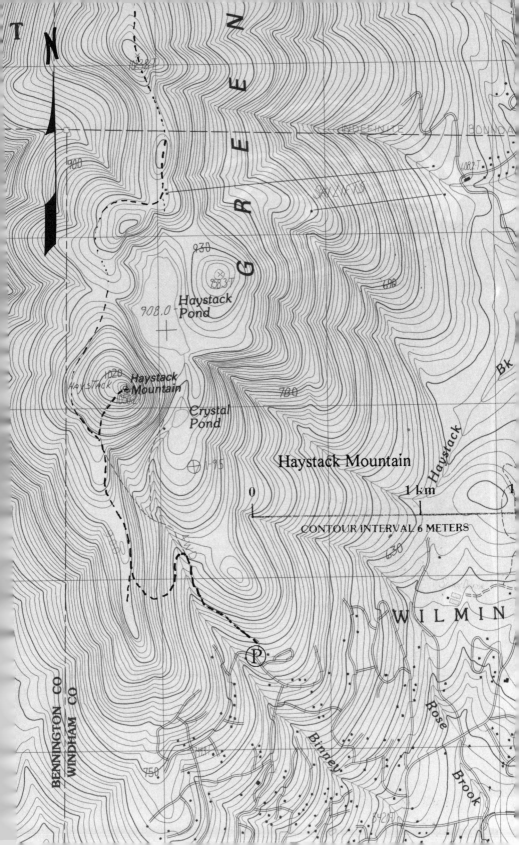

N

T N

GREEN

Haystack
Pond

908.0

Haystack
Mountain

Crystal
Pond

780

Haystack

Haystack Mountain

Bk

0   1 km

CONTOUR INTERVAL 6 METERS

630

WILMIN

BENNINGTON CO
WINDHAM CO

Rose

Binney

Brook

750

Haystack Mountain and Pond

Just at the northern edge of the clearing, Mount Snow is visible with only a small portion of its Sunbrook section showing. To the west of Mount Snow, in the far distance, is Killington, the southernmost Vermont peak over 4,000 feet in elevation. To the north is Ascutney, and solitary Monadnock is found straight to the east. If you explore the summit area you will find other vistas. On the highest rock outcrop is a brass survey marker indicating the true summit of Haystack. From one or more of these other points you will see to the south Lake Whitingham, a.k.a. the Harriman Reservoir, and the wind turbines near Searsburg. Mount Greylock with its towering monument is visible just to the west of south.

Be careful when leaving the summit. Return to the big rock slab in back of the main overlook and walk away in a straight line heading due west. Make sure you are on the trail you came up on which is marked with occasional blue markers. At the bottom of the footpath coming down from the summit, turn left and follow the trail back the way you came.

The wide woods road to which the summit path connects is called the Deerfield Ridge Trail. It is labeled this on the USGS topo map and on the Mount Snow-Haystack Ski Trail Map which adds "advanced cross-country only." It appears to be used primarily by snowmobiles. I've never skied it, but it's quite walkable during hiking season. The trail follows the spine of the narrow ridgetop, climbs and descends several smaller summits, and in places offers some views. The trail is also a major part of Mount Snow's Merrill Hiking Center. In summer, for a fee, you can take the lift to the top of Mount Snow and explore this trail and others with a special guidebook that points out various features of the mountain. Hikers should expect to see a lot of ski industry development at each end of this trail.

Mount Snow: 1,093 m, 3,586 ft.
[See Somerset Reservoir/East Branch Trail map, Chapter 6, page 144]

The summit located at the northern end of the ridge that starts with Mount Haystack is today called Mount Snow. It used to be called Somerset Mountain and Mount Pisgah, an Indian word that means "by the river." You can still see this name on some old maps. Initially, I figured that the name was changed to Mount Snow for marketing purposes because the Indian word Pisgah doesn't conjure up any up exciting images of fun and sport in the mind of the white man. But I was wrong. Mount Snow got its current name from a man who farmed its lower hillsides, Reuben Snow. Snow's old farmhouse became the Snow Barn at the ski area.

Today, Mount Snow's eastern and northern faces are scarred with ski trails and lifts. A summit lodge on top, along with countless lift towers, signs, and other structures have replaced most of the natural features that would be of interest to hikers. The natural boreal forest that once grew there has been decimated. The view from the summit lodge to the west, however, is spectacular. From there Somerset Reservoir appears to be shaped like a coiled dragon, and Glastenbury Mountain seems to rise out of a vast sea of trees.

I once took in this view at the height of the color change in early October. I've also seen it as a skier in winter. I remember teetering on my skis at the top of one of the steep runs to the north, peering out over the vast landscape. There I was, alone in awe while other skiers sped by me, scarcely aware, if at all, of the fantastic vista I was engaged with. Then an old guy, a member of the 70+ ski club, pulled up next to me and joined in the visual feast. We talked a little about the scenery, then he took off and dropped down the slope and I skated back to the eastern face of the mountain to descend on some more moderate trails.

While a large percentage of Mount Snow lies within the boundaries of the Green Mountain National Forest, the base lodge area does not. Hikers wishing to climb the mountain from there will need to make special arrangements (which means a pass and a fee) at the Merrill Hiking Center, located within the ski shop. During the summer and fall many families visit the Mount Snow Resort. While Dad plays golf, Mom and the kids can take the lift to the top and walk around. Guided hikes are possible and natural features are numbered and described in a trail book. They've even published a topographic map of the area.

It is possible to climb to the shoulder of Haystack (see page 88) and then walk the Deerfield Ridge Trail to the summit of Mount Snow, returning the way you came. Going this way, the distance from the Mount Haystack Trailhead to Mount Snow is about 5 to 6 miles, making the round trip a long day-hike.

Another possibility is to bushwhack up from the west side, off the East Branch Trail. I asked the Forest Service about the legalities of such trips, as most of the land is Forest Service land which is leased to the American Skiing Company. They told me that, if you hike to Mount Snow on the Deerfield Ridge Trail and stay on it, you're probably OK. If you step off the trail, they could ask you to leave or pay their fee. In winter the snowmobile club VAST uses this trail according to an arrangement they've negotiated with the ski area. What all this means is that Mount Snow has been more or less appropriated by winter users who favor intensive recreation. Hikers should consider these facts before climbing Mount Snow.

Stratton Mountain 1,201 m, 3,940 ft.
[See Map #2, Chapter 7, pages 158-159]

Stratton Mountain is a monadnock, which is a mountain that stands alone. It towers above the surrounding high plateau, and all of southern Vermont for that matter. At 3,940 feet, it is the highest summit in the region. Stratton is actually a double mountain in two ways. First, a lower summit of 3,490 feet stands a mile to the south, separated from the main summit ridge by a 200-foot sag. Also, the main summit itself is the southern end of a ridge along which a northern extension rises up 0.5 mile away. From Stratton Pond the mountain looks like a long, flat ridge that droops in the middle. The northern summit (3,879 feet) is where the Stratton Ski Area's skiers are brought by lift. An unmarked trail connects these two summits.

View of Stratton Mountain from Glastenbury Mountain

The Long Trail/Appalachian Trail is routed over Stratton's summit, though this wasn't always the case. The LT/AT used to cross Kelly Stand Road and head straight for Stratton Pond, while the bypass to Stratton mountain was just that, an alternate route. This was so because Stratton Mountain was owned by the International Paper Company and was only acquired by the U.S. Forest Service in 1986. The fact that the LT/AT passes over Stratton's summit today is of great significance, because this is the place where two great ideas were conceived -- the Long Trail and the Appalachian Trail.

It was on a rainy day in July of 1909 that James Paddock Taylor, stuck in his tent amongst the spruce and fir of Stratton Mountain's summit, came up with the idea of a state-wide hiking trail linking the great summits of the Green Mountains. In retrospect, it might be said that he received a vision. Taylor was a teacher who encouraged his students to hike and climb mountains. He saw these activities as important elements in one's education. The problem was that, except for Ascutney, few mountains had decent, if any, trails. Compared with the trail systems of Germany's Black Forest, which Taylor had visited a few years earlier, Vermont's Green Mountains made for some miserable hiking. Fortunately for us all, Taylor acted on his vision. The rest is history, covered already back in Chapter 2.

93

Some years later, Benton MacKaye, the father of the Appalachian Trail, had an even grander vision on Stratton Mountain. In his mind he saw the entire Appalachian range as the route of a long-distance footpath. Perhaps there's something on that summit that inspires greatness. This seems to be the case with the Stratton Ski Area which just keeps growing and growing.

The most direct way to reach Stratton's summit (with the exception of the gondola at the ski area and a 0.5 mile walk to the south on the ridge) is from Arlington-West Wardsboro Road, a.k.a. Kelly Stand Road. A large LT/AT parking area (formerly a central lumber clearing in the forest called Grout Job) is located on this road 7 miles east of Route 100. The parking area is adjacent to the East Branch of the Deerfield River, which has its source on the west side of Stratton. The hike from this parking area to the summit is not difficult, but it is not a stroll in the park either -- it's 3.5 miles to the summit with an elevation gain of 1,709 feet. Figure on about 2-to-3 hours to reach the summit. It's probably easiest to return via the same route, but there are other options discussed below.

From the parking area, begin walking south on the LT/AT. After a mile of minor ups-and-downs, you'll cross Forest Road 341, which is a major snowmobile corridor that runs along the west side of the mountain. The trail now climbs more steadily and the vegetation changes gradually. Soon enough you'll find yourself in a boreal forest of birches, spruce, and firs. The summit just south of Stratton is skirted on its west slope and then the trail drops into a col between summits before taking on the main summit. Two lookouts are passed on the way up, the first one small and nearly overgrown. After this, you pass a large boulder. The second lookout, about 0.5 mile before the summit, is better and even has some stones to sit on. Both vistas face south and offer views of Somerset Reservoir and the Haystack-Mount Snow range.

The summit of Stratton is completely covered with evergreens. There once was an old cabin here that served as home for the Green Mountain Club caretaker, but it burned. Today, there is a small clearing (no camping) and a firetower with a closed cabin on top, now considered an historic feature, that offers 360-degree views. Regarding the views, the most striking feature (to me) is the flat expanse to the west that reveals the Stratton, Bourn, and Branch ponds, as well as numerous beaver ponds and meadows. Mighty Mount Equinox in Manchester towers over the plateau in the west. The Stratton ski area lies due north along the long summit ridge; the top of the gondola line and one lift line on the east face are visible from the tower. The views in all directions are spectacular. Look for Mount Ascutney to the north-northeast and Mount Monadnock to the east, both of which stand apart from the other mountains near them.

To return, simply turn around and retrace your steps. Another option is to continue on the LT/AT which turns left (west) at the tower and descends the mountain. The downhill trail is very pleasant. There's a partially overgrown vista just below the summit and, about a mile down, a brook is crossed that is not shown on the map, a tributary of the East Branch of the Deerfield. Finally, Forest Road 341 is crossed again. One option is to turn left here and walk the road back to its junction with the LT/AT (about 2.5 miles), turn right onto the LT/AT, and walk another mile back to your car. The total distance using this loop is about 9 miles. A third option is to continue on the LT/AT from Stratton Mountain to Stratton Pond. This is described in Chapter 7, page 156.

Glastenbury Mountain: 1,142 m, 3,748 ft.
[See Map page 96 and Map #1, Chapter 7, page 154]

"In the middle of nowhere" is one way to describe this mountain, and it's true in two ways. For one thing, the town of Glastenbury no longer exists. It had a heyday of sorts during the charcoal era of the 19th century, but then it lost its population and its town status with the state of Vermont. Secondly, the summit of Glastenbury Mountain sits in the middle of a vast forest. According to the *Long Trail Guide*, the view from the tower on the summit takes in more wilderness than can be seen from any other point on the Long Trail. It's also a hard mountain to get to. Ten miles of the LT/AT, from north or south, must be covered in order to reach the summit of this mountain. That's a 20-mile round trip. It is, however, visited regularly in the winter by snowmobiles using their own trails on the eastern side of the mountain that extend to the tower on the summit.

The least complicated way to reach the summit of Glastenbury Mountain is by hiking the LT/AT north from Route 9, or south from Arlington-West Wardsboro Road. Either way, it's an overnight trip for the vast majority of hikers. The Goddard Shelter just south of the summit is the place to stay. A loop-hike from Route 9 that returns via the West Ridge Trail and Bald Mountain is also possible. This is described in Chapter 7, page 155. All these routes are hikes of over twenty miles in length.

There is another way to day-hike the summit, which is not recommended for inexperienced hikers. Also, the scenery is not quite as pretty as the LT/AT routes. You can follow Forest Road 371 (a snowmobile trail) up the mountain, bushwhack over to the LT/AT, follow it to the summit, and return the same way. The round-trip distance can then be reduced to about 10 miles -- if you can get your car onto Forest Road 325.

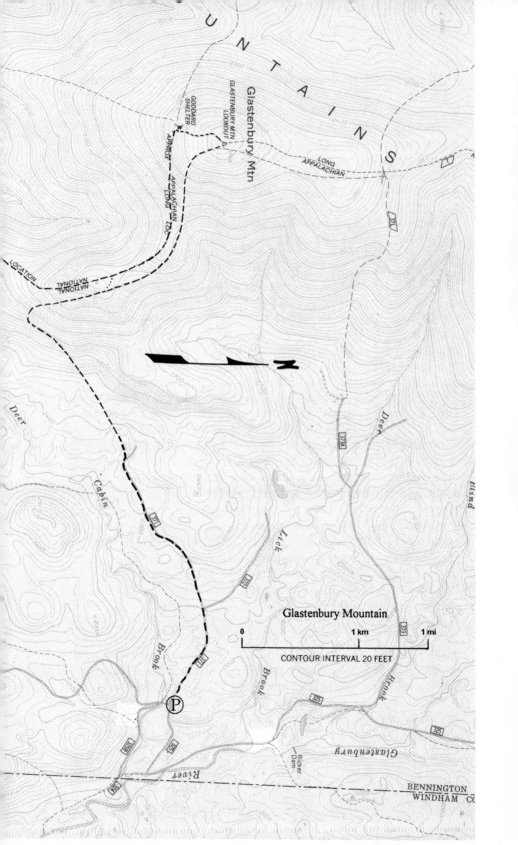

OUNTAINS

Glastenbury Mtn

GODDARD SHELTER

GLASTENBURY MTN LOOKOUT

APPROX APPALACHIAN LONG

LONG APPALACHIAN

LOCATION

NATIONAL

311

Deer

Cabin

Deer

Wind

373A

Lick

311

321

Brook

Brook

Brook

325

373

Glastenbury Mountain

0   1 km   1 mi

CONTOUR INTERVAL 20 FEET

Ⓟ

358

384

Ricker Dam

Glastenbury

325

River

324

BENNINGTON
WINDHAM CO

Some warnings about this road are in order. First, Forest Road 325, which is off Forest Road 71, is very rough, really only suitable for high clearance, 4-wheel drive vehicles. I once made it most of the way in with my 1990 Toyota Tercel by driving very, very carefully. I remember the looks on the faces of a few drivers in their big SUVs as they passed my little car way out in the middle of nowhere. Second, the forest roads are not consistently marked and can be confusing. Third, the maps of the area are not completely reliable. I've found serious errors on the USGS topographic maps. The *DeLorme's Vermont Atlas* is even worse. You need to have the USGS provisional Woodford and Mount Snow quadrangles, available from the Forest Service. The truth is, in order to hike Glastenbury by this route, you've got to be really good with maps and compass, and use plenty of good woods sense. You've been warned, so now here's how to do it:

From Route 9, 5.5 miles east of Wilmington, turn right (north) onto Forest Road 71. This dirt road is driveable for most cars. At about 6.2 miles north of Route 9, you should arrive at a junction with FR 325 (possibly unmarked) on the left, just before the bridge over the Deerfield River. If you've got a high-clearance vehicle, turn left onto FR 325, which is also snowmobile Corridor 7. (If you can't handle this road, there's another alternative listed below.) Follow FR 325 for about 4 miles, first heading west alongside Castle Brook, and then north past meadows and over small hills. The hike begins where the road crosses over Deer Cabin Brook on a bridge and then makes a sharp right turn. Park your car just over the bridge near the boulder-blocked snowmobile path (with one-way signs) on the north side of FR 325. This one-way snowmobile route is actually Forest Road 371 and you will be walking it the "wrong way" in, and the right way coming back out.

From here, follow FR 371 west on a woods road which rises slightly, then passes through an open area. A former beaver pond is passed, which may be the source of some muddy (or even flooded) parts of the path. After about 45 minutes to an hour of walking, the trail swings sharply to the right. It soon passes a road going off to the right and a swampy pond below on the left. (On the USGS Woodford topographic map, 1954, the road you pass on the right is shown as the main route, while the continuation of the trail you want to be on is shown as a dotted line.) Stay on the main trail which will swing to the left, then turn right and begin to climb. As the trail climbs higher, it turns to the left. At the top of a rise, it swings sharply to the right. Continue ahead to the top of another, smaller rise where it seems you are, more or less, on the top of a ridge. This is shown on the topo map. At this point, the snowmobile trail you are on is parallel to the LT/AT which is only about 100 yards away to the west.

Next, bushwhack to the LT/AT by taking a compass bearing and walking due west through the woods. When you come to the trail, you may want to make a careful note of where you are (so you can find it again when you return). Turn right and follow the LT/AT north for about a mile on a beautiful path, climbing stone steps, passing a spring, and arriving at the Goddard Shelter with its fine views of Mount Greylock to the south. The blue-blazed West Ridge Trail also begins here in front of the shelter and heads west and south for ten miles to Bald Mountain and Route 9. The summit of Glastenbury Mountain is 0.3 miles ahead on the LT/AT, an easy rise through a thick forest of firs. You should plan on at least three hours of hiking and a 1,650-foot vertical rise from the beginning of the hike to reach the summit. The restored firetower at the summit, with open top, has extensive views. I spent an hour here once combing the horizon with binoculars. It was a perfect autumn Sunday and I was all by myself. In fact, I didn't meet another soul the entire day. The remoteness of the area really made an impression on me.

You can return to the shelter, and follow the LT/AT to where you came, provided you remember exactly where that was. Another option, and maybe a better one, is to take the snowmobile trail which is in front of the tower all the way back. Since the snowmobile trail actually loops up to the summit, you'll want to be sure to take the south loop which will bring you (in about a mile) to where you turned off it to meet the LT/AT. If you stand in front of the tower facing east, the trail you want goes to the right, paralleling the LT/AT that you walked up on. The first mile or so passes through some very weedy areas, including some prickly plants. You will now be following the one-way trail the "right way" and will notice many signs that you probably missed on the way up. You should reach your car in about 2.5 hours of walking.

Because the snowmobile trail loops over the summit of Glastenbury Mountain, it is also possible to follow the northern leg of this trail which starts off of Forest Road 373 and then connects with Forest Road 325. A long hike from Forest Road 83 is another possibility, but I've never tried it.

If your car can't handle FR 325, you can drive (past this junction one mile further) north on FR 71, passing the campsites, and park on the left just before a gate. Here, on the other side of the brook, is unmarked FR 324 which leads in about a mile to the start of the hike described above. You should be prepared, however, for a very rough trail and the possibility of some difficult water crossings, including the Deerfield River. Only strong hikers with extensive bushwhacking experience should attempt this route.

Glastenbury's Satellite Summits

Glastenbury Mountain stands in the center of a cluster of rounded summits in the largest roadless tract of land in southern Vermont. Around it are three other summits that stand above the 1,000 meter level. One of these is Little Pond Mountain, whose elevation is shown on the USGS Woodford quad as 1,015 meters. *The Long Trail Guide*, however, calls this an unnamed peak and the lower one south of it Little Pond Mountain. Another unnamed summit due west of Glastenbury Mountain, also shown on the Woodford quad, is marked as being 1,043 meters in elevation. Since the West Ridge Trail passes just east of and below its wooded summit, I've called this West Ridge Mountain.

North of Glastenbury is yet another unnamed summit of 1,040 meters. It is shown on the Sunderland quad and is north of the Caughnawaga Shelter, named for the Caughnawaga Mohawks. This one might be called Caughnawaga Mountain, and its wooded summit is just missed by the Long Trail. This summit is located about 4.5 miles south of Kelly Stand Road, if you take the Branch Pond Trail extension to the LT/AT. There is a vista just below the summit with a view to the west that frames the mountains of the Taconic Range (Spruce Peak, Grassy Mountain, and Ball Mountain) near Arlington, Vermont. I once explored the non-descript summit of this so-called Caughnawaga Mountain in search of a tree to climb to get a view. After a few futile attempts, I gave up, finding the forested flatness of the summit to be very disorienting. It was my compass that bailed me out. Those with a sense of adventure, a map and compass, and sturdy legs may wish to explore these remote, wooded, and rounded summits.

Bromley Mountain: 1,000 m, 3,280 ft.

Bromley is the south-facing ski mountain on Routes 11 & 30. It is high enough to have a boreal forest on its summit over which the Long Trail/Appalachian Trail passes. Although the lifts and buildings of the Bromley ski area are not attractive, there is an observation platform that offers a 360-degree view. One August day, around 8 a.m., I stood on this platform and witnessed an amazing sight. All around me were clouds, and it seemed as if I were on an island sticking out of a vast white sea. Out there in the white sea were a few other "islands," Equinox, Dorset, Styles, Stratton, Glastenbury, and Snow, the "high peaks" of the southern Green Mountains. I've seen clouds below me from mountains before, but this seemed very special. Meanwhile, my son and his friend, who were both eight years old, were running around below the platform and squealing with delight, totally enchanted by all the unnatural ski apparatus.

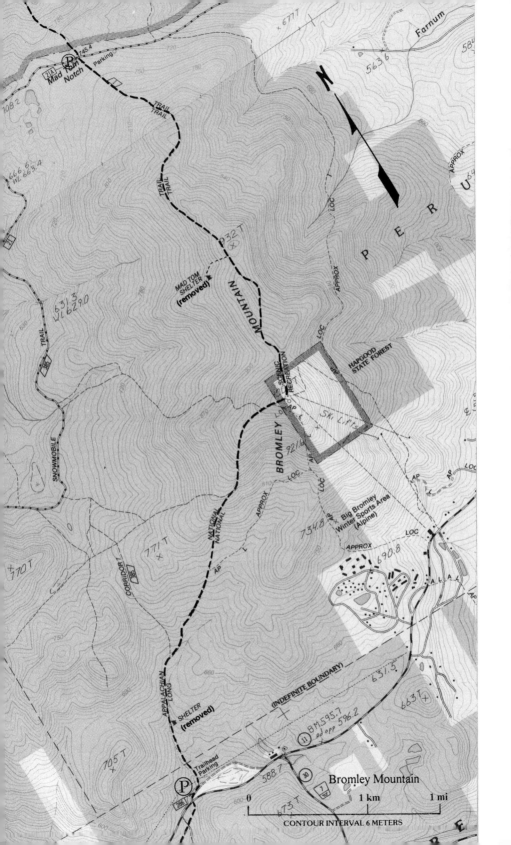

Bromley Mountain

0   1 km   1 mi

CONTOUR INTERVAL 6 METERS

North Vista from Bromley Mountain

Bromley can be climbed easily via the LT/AT, from the south or the north. The southern approach begins at the large LT/AT parking area on the north side of Routes 11 & 10 about 5.3 miles east of Manchester Center and 0.5 mile west of the junction of Routes 11 and 30. This approach is heavily used on weekends. I've seen the large parking area overflowing with cars many times.

From your car, follow the white blazes of the LT/AT ahead of you. The trail soon turns left, crosses over a brook and then a powerline. The trail now climbs, following Bromley Brook, which is to the left. You pass a tenting area, the site of a former shelter, and then a snowmobile trail, Corridor 7. About 1.5 miles into the hike, the trail becomes steeper, and at 2.3 miles it reaches a ski trail, Runaround #1, which it follows to the summit less than one-quarter mile away.

The less frequented northern approach to Bromley is from Mad Tom Notch, the gap between Bromley and Styles Peak that takes its name from Mad Tom Brook. From the junction of Routes 11 and 30, drive 3.5 miles east and turn north (left) following signs to Peru.

101

In only 0.3 mile turn left at the fork onto Hapgood Pond Road and drive another mile to a fork in the road. (Along the way you will pass the John Stark Monument, which commemorates Stark's 1777 encampment on the way to the Battle of Bennington.) Keep left at the fork and turn onto North Road (which turns to dirt). Drive another 0.8 mile to Mad Tom Notch Road, which is the second left after the fork. Mad Tom Notch Road, also Forest Road 21, is also dirt but is driveable by cars. After one mile, you'll pass a large snowmobile parking area on the right and then reach the LT/AT parking area, on the left, after 2.2 miles. There's a trail directory on the north side of the road. (This is also the starting point for the hike to Styles Peak.)

It's a 2.5-mile hike to Bromley's summit from Mad Tom Notch. The hike is enhanced by the large section of boreal forest that is traversed. Unknown to most hikers who only travel from the southern approach, Bromley has something of a north peak. This elongated northern extension, which reaches an elevation of about 3,100 feet, is high enough to support a dense evergreen forest. Near the southern edge of the small col between the two summits is a vista of Bromley's higher summit, recognizable by the ski industry apparatus sticking up from it.

Also along this northern approach, about 1.5 miles from Mad Tom Notch, is a side trail to a west-facing vista located at the site of the recently-removed Mad Tom Shelter. This shelter was once located in the notch itself. In 1980 it was disassembled and carried up the mountain to this location. I once spent a night at the Shelter's second location and remember the great views out to Equinox and Dorset mountains. I also remember hanging out with five or six Long Trail thru-hikers who were swapping stories. Thru-hikers all use special names, which are generally given to them by someone else. You can learn all about them by reading the log books that are found in every shelter.

Styles Peak: 1,034 m, 3,392 ft.
Peru Peak: 1,044 m 3,425 ft.
    [See Maps #3 and #4 in Chapter 7, pages 163, 166]

These two peaks are not as conspicuous as Bromley or the others described so far. They lie well within the mass of the Green Mountains and can't be seen from Route 7, and Bromley hides them from Routes 11 and 30. The best view of them that I've found is in the vicinity of North Landgrove, near the junction of Hapgood Pond Road and Weston Road. There they appear as a long ridge with two summits on each end. The LT/AT offers hikers access to these wilderness peaks.

Styles Peak and Peru Peak are only 1.7 miles apart and are joined by a high ridge. Both summits are also over 1,000 meters and therefore qualify to be in this section of the Chapter. Although neither summit offers extensive views, hikers will enjoy a long stretch of the unique environment of the northern boreal forest which covers their summits and the ridge between them. Many birds inhabit this summit forest during summer. A birder friend of mine sighted a variety of warblers here one June day.

Both Styles and Peru Peak fall within the boundaries of the town of Peru, hence the name of the northern, slightly higher peak. As was mentioned in Chapter 2, the name Peru replaced the original town name, Brumley, because it was thought then to evoke the glamourous qualities of South America. Styles is named for a family that farmed the eastern slopes of that mountain long ago. Both peaks also fall within the boundaries of the Peru Peak Wilderness, an odd-shaped parcel that starts at Mad Tom Notch Road and extends north to Forest Road 10. The Peru Peak Shelter, which is the closest shelter to either peak, is not at all on the mountain. It's located 1.3 miles well below the summit, and a half mile from Griffith Lake near a scenic waterfall.

Most people climb Styles Peak from Mad Tom Notch Road where LT/AT parking is available (see Bromley section, page 101). This popular day-hike is a stiff climb of about 950 feet in just 1.6 miles. At the summit is a pleasant rock ledge that offers views towards the east. Another 45 minutes of walking will take you to Peru Peak, which offers a similar view, though more modest. Peru Peak seems to receive more use, probably because of its location near Griffith Lake.

The Major Taconic Summits

Mount Equinox: 1,170 m, 3,840 ft.

Towering over the various Manchesters is mighty Mount Equinox, home to monks, towers, and a hotel. The easiest way to reach its summit is by car via Equinox Sky Line Drive, a paved toll road. There's a parking area up there for drivers and for patrons of the Equinox Mountain Inn, formerly the Sky Line Inn. Mount Equinox is within the overall boundaries of the Green Mountain National Forest, but it is not public land. Much of it is owned by the Carthusian Foundation, a monastery. The former owner and the man behind the toll road, the inn, and a number of other engineering feats, was the late Dr. Joseph B. Davidson. During the 30 years between his first purchase on the mountain and his death in 1969, he brought his mid-century vision of mountain stewardship to its present level. A small booklet called "Past and Present" offers more details about Davidson and the mountain. It's for sale at the toll house to the Sky Line Drive.

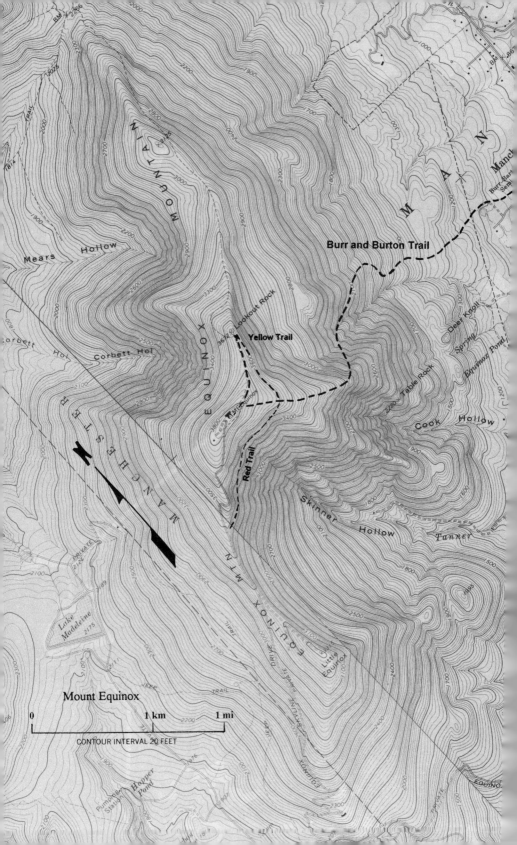

Burr and Burton Trail

Yellow Trail

Lookout Rock

Red Trail

Mears Hollow

Corbett Hol

Corbett Hol

MOUNTAIN

EQUINOX

MANCHESTER

EQUINOX MTN

Skinner Hollow

Cook Hollow

Table Rock

Deer Knoll
Spring

Tanner

Little
Equinox

Lake
Madeleine

Hopper Pond

Pumpkin
Slough

PRIVATE

JEEP

TRAIL

JEEP TRAIL

MARBLE DRIVE

MAN

Manch

Burr Burr
Spring

M A N

Mount Equinox

0   1 km   1 mi

CONTOUR INTERVAL 20 FEET

The origin of the name Equinox remains something of a mystery. Some suggest it is a corruption of the Algonkian word Owanux, which means "above us." One Vermont tradition says it was named by the first surveyor of the mountain, a Captian Partridge. On September 19, 1823, a day before the autumnal equinox, Partridge determined the elevation of the mountain to be 3,807 feet, only 33 feet from the present measurement. A 1796 map, however, has the mountain correctly located and already named Equinox. Over the years it has also been called West Mountain and Manchester Mountain.

Hikers who crave a good workout will find Equinox's Burr and Burton Trail a delight. This trail offers the highest vertical rise in the southern Green Mountains, almost 2,900 feet in just under 3 miles. The reason for this high elevation gain is that the mountain rests on the floor of the Valley of Vermont, where the elevation at the trailhead is only about 1,000 feet. In comparison, the hike up Stratton begins at an elevation of over 2,200 feet. From many Green Mountain look-outs, like Prospect Rock or the tower on Stratton, Equinox is a real monster of a mountain, and beautifully shaped. I just wish it were roadless and wild.

The Burr and Burton Trail begins in Manchester, the village, off of Route 7, at a point 1.2 miles south of its junction with Routes 11 & 30. The trailhead is at the back end of the Burr and Burton Seminary, a secondary school located just off Route 7 on the north end of the town center. From Route 7, turn west onto Seminary Avenue and drive toward the seminary buildings where the road swings to the left, then turn right onto Union Street. A quick right turn off Union Street leads to a large parking area that overlooks athletic fields. The trailhead is at the northwest end of the lot. Park your car and follow the sporadic blue markers due west.

The route is fairly simple to follow. The Burr and Burton Trail, marked with blue blazes (and also called the Equinox Trail), follows old roads that switch-back up the mountain on land preserved by the Equinox Preservation Trust. (There are also a number of trails near the base of the mountain that may be of interest to those not ready for a major climb.) The trail narrows as it rises, but the angle of rise does not change. This is a relentlessly steep trail! A cairn alongside the trail about half way up marks a short path to Equinox Spring, where water pours out of a giant white pipe.

After the spring, and plenty more climbing, the trail arrives at a non-descript junction amongst spruce and fir. Here, trail markings become more complex and confusing. A red and yellow trail heads north to Lookout Rock about 0.5 mile away. A continuation of the red trail also heads down and south, eventually reaching the toll road, though this is less evident. The Burr and Burton Trail, which by now is conspicuously lacking in blue markers, continues climbing and then reaches a tower. Turn right here and make a quick left on the yellow trail which leads in about 0.2 mile past another tower to the summit and the hotel. The last time I hiked Equinox it took me an hour to reach the spring, and another hour to reach the summit. I was in non-stop turtle gear, moving steadily, very slowly, but not breathing hard or stopping.

At the summit, there are fantastic views from the second floor of the inn, accessible by a set of outside stairs. Dorset Mountain dominates the northern direction, with the Adirondack high peaks far in the distance to the northwest. To the east, Stratton Mountain stands above all the other high summits of the southern Green Mountains. In fact, Equinox offers an excellent overview of this Chapter's subject matter. Every major summit is visible from here.

Be sure to walk out to Lookout Rock. From the summit hotel and parking area, follow the yellow trail past the tower and past the connection with the Burr and Burton Trail. On the way to Lookout Rock you'll pass an inscribed gravestone for Mr. Barbo, a dog who touched the heart of his owner, Dr. Davidson, in a way that many other dog owners, like myself, can relate to. Mr. Barbo's life was ended by a malicious hunter. There's also a laminated poem (quite emotionally intense) located here which memorializes another dog, Creamer. People place coins and other offerings on the tombstone. I was moved to tears by this scene and left a piece of chocolate there before moving on to Lookout Rock.

Lookout Rock (elevation 3,672) offers a great view of the Manchesters and an excellent view of Downer Glenn and Lye Brook Hollow. There's a bench to sit on here, as well as some open rock slabs. To return to the Burr and Burton Trail, don't retrace your steps to the summit. Keep left and follow the red markings for about 0.5 mile to that non-descript junction with the Burr and Burton Trail mentioned above. Turn left here and follow the blue markers back down, down, down to your car.

Dorset Peak: 1,1149 m, 3,770 ft.

Dorset Peak is the highest summit in a mass of mountains just south of Danby. The mountain is huge. Like Equinox, it is recognizable from many overlooks in the southern Green Mountains. Heading west on Forest Road 10, it dominates the western horizon, and it is a major horizon feature from White Rocks Mountain. Marble quarries exist on its lower flanks. It has a trail system, but most of the trails have not been kept in good condition (as of 1999). Like Stratton and Equinox, Dorset is one of New England's hundred highest peaks, and peakbaggers must climb it to achieve their goal. Although most of the Dorset Mountain mass is within the outer boundaries of Green Mountain National Forest, and a sizable portion is National Forest land, Dorset Peak itself falls just outside these boundaries.

The southern connecting ridge to Dorset Peak has several other summits. Netop Mountain (2,964 feet) is directly west of Emerald Lake. Dorset Hill is further south and tops out at 2,782. The ridge rises again, reaching Mount Aeolus at 3,230, and swings sharply west to end with 2,481-foot Owl's Head. These last two peaks have trails to their summit. Due west of Dorset Peak is 3,480-foot Dorset Mountain, not to be confused with the peak, or the hill, of the same name. Slide scars can be seen on its southern face. About sixty years ago, George Holly Gilbert built a trail system that linked all of these summits. Portions of these trails still exist, but most of them are not maintained and are recommended only to hikers with good experience in backwoods navigation.

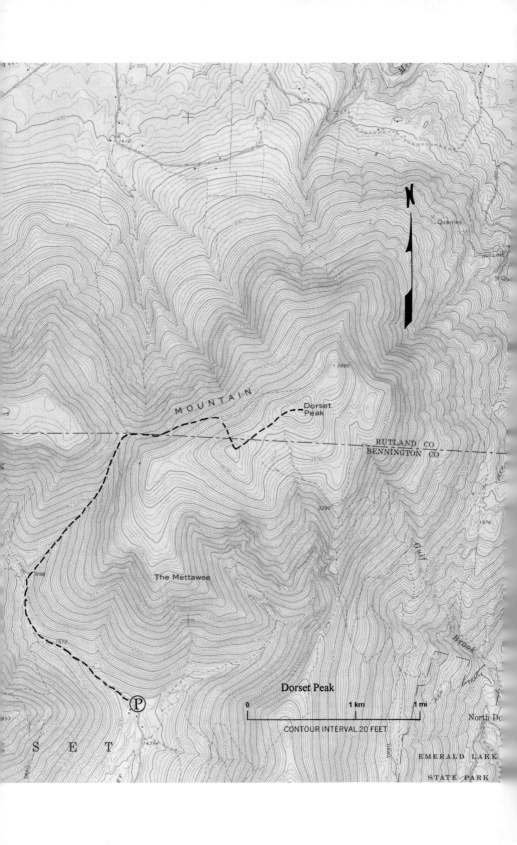

Dorset Peak

0   1 km   1 mi

CONTOUR INTERVAL 20 FEET

The trail to Dorset Peak is steep and not recommended for inexperienced hikers. It begins at the end of the public road in Dorset Hollow. From Dorset village, turn onto paved Dorset Hollow Road, turn right at the junction about 0.7 mile ahead, and keep right at a fork. The pavement ends about 1.7 miles from Dorset, but the road continues for another 2.5 miles, where it becomes Tower Road.

The hiking portion of the road begins 0.6 mile down Tower Road, past the last house on the left and just past a brook crossing (Park here but observe parking signs and respect private property). From this point, the road follows Mettawee Brook, which is on the left. Some damage from a flood in 1976 will be encountered along the way. The stream is crossed in under a mile and the trail begins to climb the mountain at a steeper pitch, eventually reaching the saddle between Dorset Mountain and Dorset Peak. From here, the trail turns east and climbs to a lower peak, where there was once a fire tower, and then turns northeast to climb the main peak. The summit is wooded.

Dorset Peak from Route 7

Peakbagging in Southern Vermont

The twelve highest summits of the southern Green Mountains and Taconic Range are 1,000 meters (3,280 feet) or higher. Here are my proposed definitions for a summit to appear on the list: A summit must be located within the outer boundaries of the Green Mountain National Forest or have a major portion of its mass be in or on Forest Service land (this excludes Okemo, a.k.a. Ludlow Mountain). An individual summit must be separated from the nearest high peak by at least one kilometer, or there must be a col between them of at least 100 meters in elevation. (This rule allows both Styles and Peru Peaks to be included.)

Some of the twelve summits listed below are not named on maps. If they have other names, I am not aware of them. "West Ridge Mountain" is what I've dubbed the flat-domed unnamed peak which is due west of Glastenbury Mountain because the West Ridge Trail passes just to the west of its true summit. Another gentle and unnamed summit north of Glastenbury, near the Caughnawaga Shelter, might be called by that Indian name which means "at the rapids" and refers to the Canadian Mohawks who periodically traveled through the area. There is also some confusion over exactly what is Little Pond Mountain (see Chapter 3, page 57). All of this peak naming and listing is unofficial, of course. I'm just making it up.

12 Highest Summits

Stratton Mountain	1,201 meters	3,940 feet
Mount Equinox	1,170	3,840
Dorset Peak	1,149	3,770
Glastenbury Mountain	1,142	3,748
Mount Snow	1,093	3,586
Haystack Mountain	1,050	3,445
Peru Peak	1,044	3,425
West Ridge Mountain	1,043	3,422
Unnamed (Caughnawaga?)	1,040	3,412
Styles Peak	1,034	3,392
Little Pond Mountain	1,015	3,330
Bromley Mountain	1,000	3,281

The Minor Summits

The Dome: 838 m, 2,748 ft.

This round-topped mountain, just over the border from Williamstown, Massachusetts, is capped by a patch of exposed rock surrounded by a healthy boreal forest. A hiking trail, which begins at the end of White Oaks Road and is maintained by the Williams Outing Club, leads to its summit. You can expect a workout as this trail climbs about 1,650 feet in 2.3 miles. From Route 7, 2.6 miles south of Route 346, turn east onto Sand Springs Road. Drive about 0.5 mile (keeping left at a fork) to White Oaks Road. Turn left here and drive another 1.5 miles to the end of the road where you can park near the trailhead. Halfway to the summit, a side trail leads steeply downhill to the Broad Brook Trail, making for a possible loop hike. Respect private property -- this hike is not entirely on public land.

The hike to the summit follows orange blazes on a wide path. At about 0.5 mile into the hike, keep left at a three-way junction. After one mile, you'll pass a junction with the Agawon Trail, which connects with the Broad Brook Trail below and makes for a loop hike. Only towards the end of the hike does the footing get rockier and the slope steeper. Near the summit, evergreens choke the trail. The last time I was there, the exposed, glacier-polished rock at the summit offered limited views, though the coolness of the boreal forest was pleasant in and of itself. I've been told that some clearing was done recently to improve the vista.

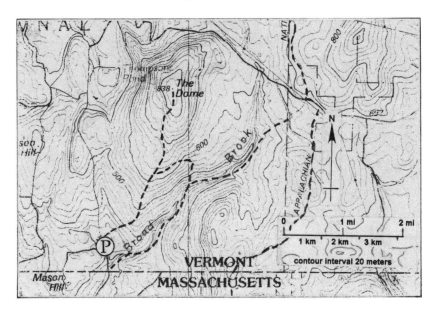

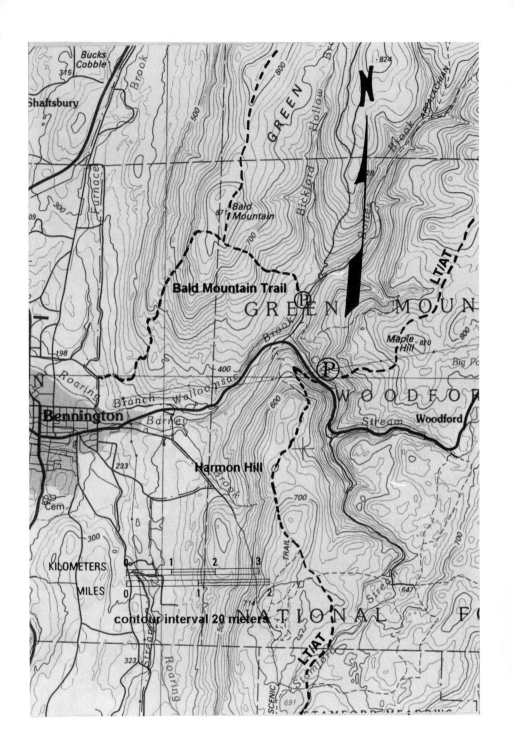

112

Harmon Hill: 709 m, 2325 ft.

Harmon Hill is the name for a broad, grassy summit to the east of Bennington. It's a friendly summit, park-like and inviting with its small rock outcrops with a good view of Bennington and its mountain, Mount Anthony. Harmon Hill is also on the Long Trail/Appalachian Trail, so it gets some use. You can expect company there on nice weekends, and other times as well. The 1,000-foot climb up is stiff at the beginning, but it's made easier by rock steps. After that climb, the route is mostly level through woods and over wet areas on boards.

A hike to Harmon Hill begins at the LT/AT parking area on Route 9, 16.4 miles west of Wilmington and 5.2 miles east of Bennington. There are actually two parking areas, one on each side of the road, but the north one is the official one. Day-hikers may wish to park on the south of Route 9. Find the LT/AT here, on the south side of Route 9, and begin hiking, or more accurately, climbing over a long series of stone steps. The climb is relentless, though switchbacks make for an easier grade. You can figure on about an hour of climbing before the rim of the gorge is reached. This edge makes a good rest stop, though the only views are through the trees.

From the edge of the gorge, the trail first descends and then climbs gradually through ferns and forest. A few wet areas are spanned by bridges. After only another half hour of walking and a slight climb, you will arrive at the broad summit of Harmon Hill. Over the years the condition of the summit has ranged from being very clear to somewhat overgrown. These changes are not natural, they are effected by the Forest Service's management plan. Controlled burns are used here from time to time for the benefit of wildlife and to retain the striking vista. On the summit, hikers will find an LT/AT sign-in and information box, as well as some signs indicating mileages. The view to the west takes in Bennington with its Battle Monument, Mt. Anthony, and the Taconic range. The return trip can take as little as an hour, though I suggest the rocky descent be done carefully.

Bald Mountain: 871 m, 2,857 ft.
[See Map, page 112]

This summit of 2,857 feet stands to the northeast of Bennington and opposite Harmon Hill. Route 9 runs alongside City Stream which has carved out the gorge between them. Bald Mountain is no longer bald. It has a healthy head of spruce and fir growing on its top that is now blocking what were once spectacular views. It still receives a moderate amount of use because it is accessible from Bennington, and it is located at a junction of trails. Near the actual summit is a large cairn and some campsites.

The Bald Mountain Trail starts in Bennington, climbs to within 0.1 mile of the true summit, and then descends to Woodford Hollow. Even though it is said to be one of the oldest trails in the area, this trail is not very well maintained. It is certainly not heavily used. Its eastern end, however, is a leg in the Glastenbury Mountain circuit described in Chapter 7, page 155.

The Bennington end of the Bald Mountain Trail starts near a turn on North Branch Street, northwest of the town center. There is a utility line cut running through this area also. North Branch Street can be accessed from either Route 7 north of town, or Route 9 about 0.7 mile east of the town center (junction of Routes 7 and 9). From Route 9 take North Branch Street north, turn right onto North Branch Street Extension, and cross over a bridge.

The trailhead, with very limited parking (maybe three cars at the most), is about 0.5 mile ahead on the right at a bend in the road. From this trailhead, it is four miles to the summit. The trail, which suffers some ATV damage, does offer views on the way up of Bennington and its environs from an area that was once a rockslide. The elevation gain on this approach is considerable, 2,150 feet.

The eastern end of the Bald Mountain trail is located in Woodford Hollow on the west side of Harbour Road (which is the same as Woodford Hollow Road) about 0.7 mile north of Route 9. Harbour Road (dirt and gravel) turns north off Route 9 about 1.2 miles west of the LT/AT crossing and 3.2 miles east of Branch Street in Bennington (or four miles from the town center). The Town of Woodford's municipal building, which looks like a chapel, is located at this corner. The trailhead is found just to the right of a large, concrete water tank and it utilizes a driveway (do not park on it or block it) for only 100 yards before the trail veers left into the woods.

From Woodford Hollow, it is only two miles and a vertical rise of 1,580 feet to the summit of Bald Mountain. The first 0.5 mile of trail requires constant attention to markers because it wanders through a wet area criss-crossed with ATV trails. A sign-in register is located in this area. The route to the summit is completely wooded, with only partial views through the trees to be found just below the summit. The last quarter mile or so of the climb is via switchbacks through evergreens. Just before this section, a sign marks a trail that supposedly leads to a spring called Bear Wallow, though I couldn't find it.

One beautiful winter day I snowshoed to the summit and found the upper section of the trail stunning. The trees were laden with fresh snow, their boughs hanging over the trail waiting to drop their load on me as I passed by. Just before the summit, I looked out to the east and saw the top of Little Pond Mountain glaring white with ice. At the junction with the West Ridge Trail, in the midst of frosted firs, I smelled gasoline and then found three men on three snowmobiles. I said "Hi" and turned right toward the actual summit. It was obvious they had come that way. Their route was marked by a path of packed snow about five feet wide and several small trees that were flattened and torn. I waved to them again as they passed by and plowed down the steep north slope of Bald Mountain. A ranger later told me that they shouldn't have been there.

Mount Aeolus: 985 m, 3,230 ft.

This southern summit of the Dorset Peak ridge has a route, consisting of old quarry roads and a footpath, to its summit. Along the way, and at the summit, are views of the Green Mountains and the Valley of Vermont. The trail is 2.7 miles long, with an 1,850-foot elevation gain. Mount Aeolus was named for the Greek god of the winds by students of the Amherst College geology professor Edward Hitchcock (one of the great pioneers of dinosaur paleontology). Apparently, it was named so because of the high winds he and his students experienced that day. The myth of Aeolus says he was closed up in a cave by Zeus and (By Jupiter!) Mount Aeolus has its own cave! Today, the cave is gated to prevent any disturbance of the endangered Indiana bats that live there.

To reach the Mount Aeolus Trail from Route 7A, turn west onto Morse Hill Road. This turn is about a mile south of East Dorset and 0.3 mile south of the Routes 7 and 7A junction. After going 1.2 miles west on Morse Hill Road, turn right (north) onto Dorset Hill Road, which will soon become dirt. (This road is shown as Quarry Road on some maps.) The trailhead, which is an old road on the left, is 1.9 miles from this turn. Park here, being respectful of the private homes in the vicinity.

The trail to the summit of Mount Aeolus is not officially marked or maintained, but snowmobile arrow markers and orange surveying tape, plus common sense, will lead experienced hikers there. Begin by walking west on the old road and then turning left (south), through a gate, and onto a gravel utility road. After a gradual climb of about a mile, the trail passes an old quarry stonepile on the right and then arrives at a junction. Continue straight ahead on a dirt path.

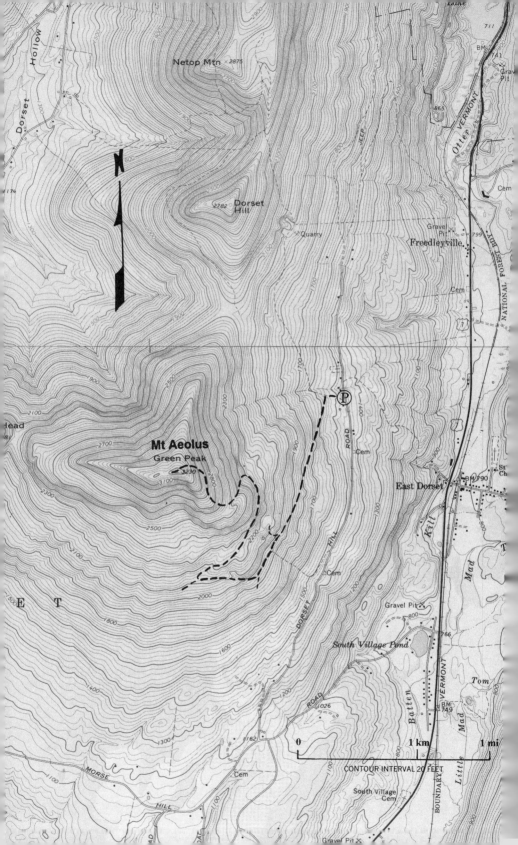

Another few minutes of walking brings you to another fork. Keep right here and walk uphill to the remains of a very old quarry, said to be the first marble quarry in the country. There are a number of viewpoints in this vicinity that reveal the wall of the Green Mountains and the Valley of Vermont. Where the trail forks again, keep left. (A right turn leads onto the floor of the quarry where, one spring day, I found a profusion of wild columbine flowers blooming among the rocks.)

The trail, now grassy, continues to wind its way uphill, passing above the quarry and through an area where the Indiana bat is protected. Keep right at a junction and continue climbing to a fork. To your right is a flat area with a limited view. (Better views are had by backtracking about 100 yards and turning onto a faint footpath near a rock wall. Be careful here, the path leads to some very steep ledges.)

To continue the hike to the summit, bear left at this fork. The trail, now shrinking in size, winds through the woods, swings to the southeast of the peak, and then begins to climb very steeply. The boreal forest is reached in this area, but the trail becomes very difficult to follow in places. Look for survey ribbon and try to remember your route -- you may need to use this information on your way back down. After a few false summits, the real one is reached. A pile of rocks, an iron rod, and some yellow paint mark the approximate summit and a junction of abandoned trails.

About 100 feet before reaching this marker, you may have spotted a small rock ledge, about 30 feet south of the path, that offers a great view of Stratton, Mount Snow, Glastenbury, and Equinox. On the trip back down, you may find a few other minor vistas that you missed on the way up. (Since my last hike here, I was told that a wide, 180-degree vista is to be found about one-quarter mile west of the summit, along the descending summit ridge.)

Owl's Head: 756 m, 2,481 ft.
[See Map page 118]

Owl's Head can be reached via a 2.2-mile trail that is not recommended for inexperienced hikers. The trail is lightly marked, it is not maintained, and crosses private land (please respect landowner's rights). This rocky knob offers good views to the south and west from Gilbert Lookout, named for Dorset Mountain's trailbuilder.

To get there, take Route 30 for about 1.5 miles north of South Dorset Village and look for Kelly Road on the north side of Route 30, immediately west of the Norcross Marble Quarry. Turn onto Kelly Road and look for roadside parking. From where you've parked, you have to walk the gravel Black Rock Road north for a quarter mile, bear right at a fork, then turn right onto a wooded lane opposite the second house on the left.

You will come to a deserted camp, turn left here and look for yellow flag markers. The markers lead you uphill to an interesting marble quarry, the Gettysburg Quarry, where the gravestones for the dead of that Civil War battle are said to have been cut. At the quarry, the trail swings to the right and climbs gradually to the top of a small knoll just west of Owl's Head. The trail then descends into a saddle, passes a large boulder, and then climbs Owl's Head on a steep, narrow path. The Gilbert Lookout is a small ledge along the trail just below the summit.

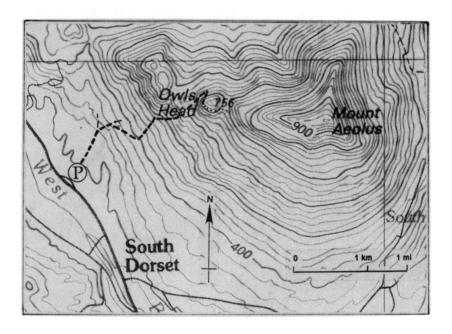

Baker Peak: 866 m, 2,840 ft.   *[See Map #4 in Chapter 7, page 166]*

At 2,840 feet, Baker Peak may not seem high, especially in comparison to monsters like nearby Dorset. But Baker Peak sports the most expansive ridge-like ledges in the southern Green Mountains. Glastenbury and Stratton have their towers, while Haystack, Equinox, and Styles have lookouts, but Baker has a strip of basement rock that makes you feel like you're on the summit of a real mountain. The view out to Dorset Peak is quite fine, too. It doesn't matter that this strip of ledge is not the true summit of the mountain, or more accurately, the highest elevation in the vicinity. It feels like a mountain ridge and because it does, it attracts many day-hikers.

The Long Trail/Appalachian Trail runs right over Baker Peak. From Big Branch, it's about 5 miles south, with two shelters in between. Most people, however, climb it from Danby via the Lake Trail. The Lake Trail is the old carriage road that brought guests to the Griffith Hotel which once stood on the west shore of Griffith Lake. It's graded, makes a giant switchback, and offers a few views along the way. The Lake Trail begins one-half mile down South End Road, which becomes Forest Road 259. This road is on the east side of Route 7, 2.2 miles south of Mount Tabor Road in Danby. You'll pass over the railroad tracks and go by a cemetery on your way to the trailhead. At the start, the trail first follows a brook, then switches back sharply to the left and enters the Big Branch Wilderness. As the road climbs, it passes a steep rock face, the trail originally held up by trestles. Where the trail rounds the corner of a ravine, a side trail on the right leads up to a vista. Ahead, the Lake Trail follows McGinn Brook, crossing it at its junction with the Baker Peak Trail. Hikers aiming for the peak will turn left onto this mile-long trail which follows an old logging road, then climbs a rocky path to the peak. The total distance from trailhead to peak is 2.9 miles with a vertical rise of 2,118 feet.

Many hikers walking the Lake Trail to Baker Peak also take in Griffith Lake. In my opinion, the best way to climb Baker Peak is by the Baker Peak Trail, not the LT/AT heading north from Griffith Lake. Hikers coming from this direction will experience the bare ridge as more of a ledge and overlook. From the Baker Peak Trail, the ridge feels more like a summit, and I like it that way. I have a memory of sunning myself on the rocks one unusually warm December afternoon, Dorset Mountain looming in front of me. My friend and I noticed the reddish haze on the horizon and decided to call it "corrupted air," in keeping with the 19th-century theme of carriage road and hotel guests. Later that night, my friend had what seemed to be a case of the 19th-century lady's disease, "the vapors." The haze, of course, was just some 20th century pollution drifting eastward.

Atop Baker Peak

Green Mountain: 762 m, 2,500 ft.
[See Map #5 in Chapter 7, page 169]

Green Mountain is a minor ridge on the generally north-south-running wall of the Green Mountains east of Route 7. It's just to the northeast of Danby, north of the gorge cut by Big Branch. Why it is named Green Mountain is not clear. Perhaps it acquired this name because it was covered with evergreens at a time when other mountains were either stripped of forest or covered with a second growth of hardwoods.

The easiest way to climb Green Mountain is to hike north for about two miles on the LT/AT from Forest Road 10 at Big Branch. Then, at Little Rock Pond, take the northern end of the Green Mountain Trail up to the ledges that are less than a mile away. The Green Mountain Trail traverses this mountain, and using that section of the LT/AT, a loop hike is possible. This is described in Chapter 7, page 168.

To find the LT/AT parking area for Little Rock Pond and the Green Mountain Trail, turn east off Route 7 at Mount Tabor. This turn, marked Brooklyn Road, is about 12.5 miles north of the junction of Route 7 and Routes 11 and 30. There's a lumber depot and gas station at this turnoff. (Turning west here will lead directly to Danby.) Following National Forest signs to Big Branch, drive 3.2 miles to the Long Trail/Appalachian Trail parking area which will be on your right. Along the way you will enter the Green Mountain National Forest where the road becomes Forest Road 10. There is also a hairpin turn on the way and the Big Branch Picnic Area, which offers a vista over the ravine created by Big Branch Brook.

The Green Mountain Trail is found just west of the LT/AT parking area on Forest Road 10. It grazes the Big Branch picnic area (another possible place to park), and then swings to the north. From the trailhead, it is about 3.6 miles to the mountain's high point, with a few westward viewpoints located along the way. This section of the trail is mostly on woods roads, but after reaching the top of the long ridge, it becomes a footpath. The best views from the summit are 100 yards off the main trail just east of where the trail swings over the main ridge.

The rocky eastern face of Green Mountain overlooks beautiful Little Rock Pond. A few overlooks on and just off the Green Mountain Trail offer good views of the pond and the nearby mountains to the north, west, and south. This section of the trail is within a mile of Little Rock Pond and features some scrambling over ledges. I've enjoyed this little gem of a trail several times in trips to Little Rock Pond, scrambling up there in as little time as 20 minutes. These "summit" ledges can also be reached via the Homer Stone Trail from South Wallingford.

White Rocks Mountain:
North summit 796 m, 2,611 ft.
South summit: 806 m, 2,644 ft.
[See Chapter 6, Map for Wallingford Pond, page 137]

This mountain, which looks so dramatic from the Parapet on the White Rocks Trail below it, is a continuation of the western escarpment of the Green Mountains. Green Mountain itself is just to the south, separated from White Rocks Mountain by the ravine carved by Homer Stone Brook. The sharp cliff, called White Rocks Cliff, appears to be a summit when seen from below, but it is not. Due to the endangered status of the peregrine falcon, this and other trails near White Rocks Cliffs may be closed from time to time.

White Rocks Mountain from the Ice Beds Trail

The actual summit of White Rocks Mountain is wooded and reachable only by bushwhack. It is probably the southerly, and higher, of the two summits shown on topographic maps of the area. At least one map has labeled the lower summit as White Rocks Mountain. Neither summit has a trail, though the LT/AT passes near to both. Two trails in the vicinity should be noted, however. An old trail does leave the LT/AT and descends to an overlook at the top of the cliffs, which appear from below to be the mountain itself. This trail may be closed to protect the falcons. The Keewaydin Trail, also subject to occasional closure, climbs from the picnic area to the LT/AT just north of the summit.

Hikers may also wish to walk the Ice Beds Trail from the White Rocks Picnic Area. From Wallingford, drive 2.1 miles west on Route 140, bear right at the fork onto Sugar Hill Road, then immediately turn right. Signs will lead you to parking, the picnic area, and the trailheads for the Ice Beds Trail and the Keewadin Trail. The Ice Beds Trail climbs a small but very rocky ridge that offers excellent views of White Rocks Mountain. It then descends and swings around to a boulder field where ice may be trapped well into the summer, keeping the area very cool.

Chapter 6

Hiking to the Ponds

A major feature of the southern section of the Green Mountain National Forest are its many ponds and reservoirs. Some of these are pristine, accessible only by hiking. A few of the ponds at higher elevations, such as Stratton Pond and Bourn Pond, have bog-like qualities and are of interest to naturalists. In contrast to these more isolated bodies of water are several ponds with road access and two huge reservoirs. A few trails exist along the shorelines of these ponds and reservoirs which offer hikers the opportunity to explore less frequented areas. Finally, there are the numerous beaver ponds that dot the high Green Mountain plateau. Most of these ponds are difficult to reach, requiring a strenuous bushwhack through dense growth and wetland.

The Hiker's Ponds

Stratton Pond
[See Map #2 in Chapter 7, pages 158-159]

The westward view from the tower on Stratton Mountain is one of an extensive wilderness, dotted with ponds and bounded ten miles distant by the mass of Mount Equinox. In the middle of this vast perspective is Stratton Pond, the largest body of water on this high southern Green Mountain plateau. Farther west is Bourn and Branch Ponds. About half of this pond-speckled area is a legal wilderness, the Lye Brook Wilderness, which includes Bourn Pond but not Branch Pond or Stratton Pond. Astute observers with good maps will notice many other small ponds where clearings should be, or meadows where ponds are shown on the map. These are ephemeral ponds, created by beaver. These busy rodents dam the streams, live there for a few years, and then move on. The flooded streams kill the trees, and when the dam breaks and the stream reverts to its original bed, a clearing is left behind. Map makers just can't keep up with the beavers.

Stratton Pond is one of the most popular hiking and backpacking destinations in the southern section of Green Mountain National Forest. The Long Trail/Appalachian Trail passes along part of its shoreline, bringing in a steady stream of hikers. *The Long Trail Guide* says that it receives the heaviest annual overnight use of any location on the entire 270-mile trail.

Thankfully, a Green Mountain Club caretaker resides at Stratton Pond between Memorial Day and Columbus Day and keeps things under control. He or she will collect a fee from each camper. If it were not for the caretaker's presence, the pristine condition of this over-used area would probably deteriorate rapidly. Stratton Pond is also the largest body of water along the Long Trail. It is said to be 30 feet deep in places and is big enough for whitecaps to form under high winds.

Stratton Pond is located far enough from the nearest road to be spared overuse by non-hiking tourists. The shortest route there is the Stratton Pond Trail which comes in from Arlington-West Wardsboro Road, also called Kelly Stand Road. A parking area for this trail is located on the north side of Arlington-West Wardsboro Road, eight miles west of Route 100. The blue-blazed Stratton Pond Trail is a four-mile jaunt across a high forested plateau through sections of forest that were logged not that long ago. It's a two-hour or more walk with full packs.

Stratton Pond

The trail begins at an elevation of 715 meters (2,346 feet), rises to 831 meters (2,732 feet), and descends to the pond which lies at about 780 meters (2,559 feet). About two-thirds of the way from the parking area to the pond, you will cross Forest Road 368.12. This is actually a snowmobile route that meets Arlington-West Wardsboro Road at a point very near to the LT/AT trailhead parking for Stratton Mountain. Since this is a snowmobile trail, it is not well drained and is not recommended for hikers. On the Stratton Pond Trail, north of this junction, a low point in the hike is reached which may hold snow late into the spring. As of 1999, the Vondell Shelter, the last of three shore-line shelters, has been removed.

I've had some wonderful experiences at Stratton Pond. A few years ago, a friend and I spent a night at the Bigelow Shelter, which was located right on the shoreline. While preparing our dinner, rather quietly as I recall, a large beaver swam up to us, smacked his tail hard on the water, turned around and swam back out into the pond. I guess he told us a thing or two. The shelter is now gone, removed due to old age, and when a new one is built, it will be located farther from the water's edge. Mr. Beaver will no doubt be pleased with this change.

Approaching Stratton Pond from Stratton Mountain on the LT/AT, west of Forest Road 341, a low point is crossed where there are several meadows. To the north is a small pond, and to the south there are former beaver ponds that have left large meadows and the remnants of a beaver lodge. After a short climb, the trail then descends to a junction with the Stratton Pond Trail. A right turn here leads to the pond in 200 yards or so. From this point, the location of the GMC caretakers camp, there are footpaths that encircle the pond. To the right, on the LT/AT, the path crosses over a bridge. This area shows the pond to have bog-like qualities. Nearby is a healthy patch of pitcher plants that get necessary nutrients lacking in the acidic soil by trapping insects and digesting them in their pouch-like leaves.

One warm autumn day I hiked into Stratton Pond with two friends who had never before visited the Green Mountains. They are White Mountain hikers, used to steep climbs, alpine summits, and full-service huts. For them, the hike into the pond was a stroll in the park. Upon reaching the pond, however, they were impressed by an outstanding natural feature. A bare-breasted woman, who was marveling at the beauty of the pond, turned to greet us and initiated a short conversation. My friends remarked that this was not something they had previously experienced in any of their White Mountain journeys.

Bourn Pond

[See Map #2 in Chapter 7, pages 158-159]

Bourn Pond lies due west of Stratton Pond and is connected to it by the Lye Brook Trail. Certain aspects of this pond, particularly the trails that meet near it, have already been discussed in Chapter 4, page 76. Like its close neighbor Stratton Pond, it has bog-like qualities. Very little of its shoreline is lined with rocks, most of it consisting of thick plant colonies, including the carnivorous pitcher plant and the tiny sundew.

Bourn Brook drains north from the Pond, passes the William B. Douglass Shelter on the LT/AT and then turns west. It then drops over the edge of the high plateau into Downer Glenn, on whose northern lip Prospect Rock stands out. Finally, it flows into Manchester to join the Batten Kill just south of Manchester Center. Both the Brook and the Pond were named for a Manchester family who in 1819 became involved in one of the best known murder trials of the day (see Chapter 2, page 37).

Although it is generally not as heavily used as Stratton Pond, Bourn Pond does get a good share of visitors, especially on summer weekends. On weekdays, however, it may be deserted. I once spent a Thursday night in August at the South Bourn Shelter with a friend and her fat dog, Hura Humba. We walked in on the Branch Pond Trail and arrived late in the afternoon. I was surprised to see that we were the only ones there. At dusk I walked down to the pond to witness the silent cruise of a large blue heron just a few feet over the water. It alighted on the top of a large dead tree along the west shore. There was a sense of the prehistoric in that flight, the subtle flapping of the wings, the long neck, and the legs hanging back suggested a pterodactyl, not a modern bird. Thankfully, there were no biting flies that night and a chorus of frogs began as the light dimmed.

Later that night we walked back down to the shoreline to study the sky and hopefully see what the annual Perseid meteor shower might bring us. We saw a few meteorites, but were also subjected to the sight and sound of at least a dozen private planes, probably landing at Manchester airport just a few miles to the west. We wondered about whether the Forest Service has the power to reduce noisy air traffic flying over this wilderness. In other words, does "wilderness protection" extend to the air space above the physical land boundaries of a wilderness area?

Noise pollution is a complicated issue and is not clearly defined by law. It is more a matter of interpretation (the "spirit of the law") rather than the "letter of the law." The 1964 Wilderness Act defines "wilderness" as an area "untrammeled by man...retaining its primeval character and influence, (with) outstanding opportunities for solitude." It is this term "solitude" that has been interpreted to mean natural quiet. In 1987, Congress passed Public Law 100-91, which did not call for the reduction of noise, but only required the Forest Service and the National Park Service to conduct studies of aircraft impact on wilderness areas and parks. After much bureaucratic busywork, the resulting report of 1992 concluded that, "Few adverse impacts to wilderness users were found resulting from aircraft overflights of Forest-Service-managed wildernesses. The worst case found was a fairly small percentage of wilderness visitors who experienced varying degrees of noise-induced annoyance." We have to wonder who took part in these "studies" -- Perhaps a large percentage of snowmobilers, SUV-owners, or other mechanized users so over-exposed to noise that they do not know the value of quiet?

Numerous other studies have shown the detrimental impact of aircraft noise, including the fact that overflights are highly disruptive to the feeding, breeding and nesting patterns of wildlife, as well as being disturbing to hikers, naturalists, and other non-motorized users and self-reliant people of peace. With the lack of national restrictions on noise pollution, however, the issue of noise abatement must be painstakingly addressed one area at a time, as in the recent case of air flights over the Grand Canyon. It all comes back to the same old battle called "user conflicts."

I have other memories of that night at Bourn Pond. Our companion dog Hura Humba, part Black Lab and part Chow, alternately slept and guarded the shelter. The sleeping part was mostly fine, except when she was snoring, but her guarding behavior drove me crazy. Throughout the night she would get up, snort at any sound coming from the forest, and then she would pace, the nails on her paws making clicking sounds on the floor boards of the shelter. I was glad we were alone in the shelter because I would have never subjected anyone else to that kind of torture. Needless to say, no wild animals, not even the ubiquitous shelter mice, dared to come near us that night.

Bourn Pond can be reached from all the four cardinal directions, which seem to converge at a non-specific point near the shelter. One approach is via the Lye Brook Trail (7.3 miles), described in Chapter 4, page 76.

Another way to get to Bourn Pond is via the north-south Branch Pond Trail. Approaching the Pond from the north on the LT/AT, the pond is four miles south on the Branch Pond Trail (and 4.9 miles south of Prospect Rock).

From the south it is 4.3 miles from Arlington-West Wardsboro Road. This trailhead, which is unmarked and offers only very limited parking, is located 9.3 miles west of the junction of Route 100 and Arlington-West Wardsboro Road/Kelly Stand Road (2.2 miles west of the Stratton Pond Trail parking area). A short cut to the Branch Pond Trail is found at the end of Forest Road 70, which turns north from Arlington-West Wardsboro Road 11.2 miles west of Route 100. A two-mile drive down Forest Road 70 leads to a parking area and a connector trail, about one-quarter mile long, that leads to the Branch Pond Trail. From there it is 2.5 miles to the Bourn Pond.

Finally, Bourn Pond can also be reached from Stratton Pond on the Lye Brook Trail (2 miles).

Griffith Lake
[See Maps #3 and #4 in Chapter 7, pages 163, 166]

Griffith Lake evokes a strong sense of wildness. It's a large pond, about 16 acres, that is surrounded by two official wilderness areas, although it is open to motorized snow touring all winter. Camping is restricted to a designated campsite on its east shore and the Peru Peak shelter just a half mile to the south of the lake. Not that long ago, Griffith Lake, formerly called Buffum Pond, was buzzing with activity. There's a open area on its west shore where a clubhouse-hotel once stood. After the age of lumbering, a number of hunting camps and lodges were established in the area around the lake. I've been told that one still exists. Still, the lake has always seemed remote and distant to me. Moose sightings are common in the area.

Griffith Lake is named for Silas L. Griffith, Vermont's first millionaire. Before the coming of the Long Trail, the vast forests in the vicinity of this lake and Little Rock Pond were lumbered, mostly by Griffith. He was born in 1837 in Danby, Vermont, and as a youth became a clerk in a local general store. It was during the financial panic of 1857 that he gained some experience as a logger in Buffalo, New York, but he came back to Danby when he was able to borrow funds to set up his own store. Griffith's store was a success and he rapidly became one of the leading businessmen in his town.

128

Griffith Lake

After ten years as a store owner, Griffith acquired some timber land as payment for a debt, and this marked his entrance into the lumber business. Selling lumber was only one of several forest opportunities that Griffith took advantage of. Another was charcoal. At the time, charcoal was in great demand and Griffith made a deal with an iron-making company in Lime Rock, Connecticut, to supply them with charcoal. Apparently, the supply of wood was running out in Connecticut, and shipping charcoal made in Vermont to fire Connecticut's furnaces was profitable. Conveniently for Griffith, a rail line already existed at Danby. Perfectly positioned between his buyer and his acres of forest, Griffith was ready to exploit the forest and make some really big money.

For several years, Griffith ran the largest individually-owned business in Vermont. His 50,000+ acres of land boasted nine sawmills and six general stores. He sold lumber and using all parts of the harvested trees, built boxes and made charcoal. He even found a market for the sawdust. Griffith, now a real millionaire, built a large and interesting house in Danby, which is today the Silas Griffith Inn. He also built a summer home on Griffith Lake. In 1930 his forests around Little Rock Pond were acquired by the Forest Service, and in 1984 portions were designated a wilderness and part of the White Rocks National Recreation Area.

Hikers can reach Griffith Lake from several directions. From Route 7 in Danby, the Lake Trail switchbacks up the ridge, follows McGinn Brook for a ways, then makes another long switchback before arriving at the Lake. This route, which was originally the carriage road to Griffith's lake house, is also the approach to Baker Peak described in Chapter 5, page 119. It involves a climb of roughly 600 meters or 2,000 feet in 3.5 miles. A parking area for the Lake Trail is located on a small road (South End Road or Town Highway 5) that turns east off of Route 7, about 2.2 miles south of Danby. After a railroad crossing and a cemetery is the parking area, about one-half mile from Route 7. The trail starts at the end of the parking area heading east. After about 0.7 mile the trail makes a switchback to the left, climbs in front of a rock face, then turns right and east again, now following the side of a ravine. Look for a side trail that leads to a vista here. The trail continues in an easterly direction, now following McGuinn Brook. It crosses over several small tributaries, passes a junction with the Baker Peak Trail, then swings to the right and up to Griffith Lake. Just before the lake, the trail joins the Long Trail/Appalachian Trail.

Another route is via the Old Job Trail from the end of Forest Road 30. From Danby, drive east on Forest Road 10 for 7.7 miles (past the LT/AT parking area), and turn right onto Forest Road 30. About 2.3 miles ahead, at the end of the road, is the trailhead and limited parking. This wide trail, which is a snowmobile route, follows Lake Brook, the drainage from Griffith Lake, for much of its distance. It's an easier walk in than from the Lake Trail, with a 200-meter (650-foot) elevation gain in about 3.5 miles. It can be muddy, however.

Two approaches to Griffith Lake from the south are also possible. One is off Forest Road 21 via the LT/AT south from Mad Tom Notch, a distance of about 5 miles. Directions to this trailhead are found in Chapter 5 in the section on Styles Peak and Peru Peak (page 102), both of which must be climbed before the trail descends to the lake.

Another route is from Porky Point, the parking area near the end of Forest Road 58. This parking area's name derives from the many porcupines who have been known to chew up important hoses on the underside of parked automobiles, leaving them undriveable. Forest Road 58 turns north from Forest Road 21 about a half mile past the LT/AT parking at Mad Tom Notch, passing an outstanding overlook on its way to the parking area. The roughly two-mile walk to the lake from this parking area is on a dirt road/snowmobile corridor. It's not particularly scenic and is often muddy. As part of a circular loop, this route is described in Chapter 7, page 162.

Little Rock Pond
[See Map #5 in Chapter 7, page 169]

Due north of Griffith Lake is Little Rock Pond, a small gem in the White Rocks National Recreation Area of the Green Mountain National Forest. Its crystal clear waters reveal both a rocky bottom and the reflection of Green Mountain which rises over its western shore. A tiny island near its northern shore adds to its overall charm. Little Rock Pond feels more comforting to me than lonesome Griffith Lake, probably because of its small size.

It's easy to hike to Little Rock Pond because Forest Road 10 climbs up to nearly the same elevation as the pond. Of course, this means that the area is popular. A large parking area has been built where the LT/AT crosses the road, and a massive, handicapped-accessible outhouse stands aside the trail as it enters the woods. This modern outhouse is so huge it could probably serve as an emergency shelter for ten people in winter. In spite of all this attention, the pond and its environs are spotless, mostly due to the efforts of the Green Mountain Club. During hiking season, Memorial Day to Columbus Day, the GMC sponsors a caretaker who lives in a tent near the pond. The caretaker collects a small fee from campers who use the area ($5 in 1998), keeps a watch on happenings, and is always available to answer questions from hikers and campers.

The trail to Little Rock Pond is the LT/AT heading north which follows brooks through forest once owned by Silas Griffith. There are a few mounds of black dirt, along with some bricks, in the first part of the hike to the pond, these being the remains of some of Griffith's charcoal kilns. Charcoal is made by stacking cut wood in a pile, covering it with dirt, leaving a small opening at the top, and setting it on fire. The fire is left smoldering inside the mound for a week or two and then the top hole is covered, putting out the fire. Later the charcoal is collected.

To find the LT/AT parking area for Little Rock Pond, turn east off Route 7 at Mount Tabor. This turn, labeled Brooklyn Road, is about 12.5 miles north of the junction of Route 7 and Routes 11 and 30. There's a lumber depot and gas station at this turnoff. (Turning west here will lead directly to Danby.) Following National Forest signs to Big Branch, drive a total of 3.2 miles to the Long Trail/Appalachian Trail parking area which will be on your right. Along the way you will enter the Green Mountain National Forest where the road becomes Forest Road 10. There is also a hairpin turn on the way and the Big Branch Picnic Area, which offers a vista over the ravine created by Big Branch Brook.

131

Little Rock Pond

The hike to Little Rock Pond is just over two miles -- easy for the most part, but rocky in places. The trail first follows Little Black Brook, crossing it at one point on a steel beam. Ahead, a few wet areas are covered with planks, then the trail rises and becomes steadily rockier. A side trail to the Lula Tye Shelter is passed about one-quarter mile before the pond. This shelter was formerly located alongside the pond where the Green Mountain Club (GMC) caretaker is now stationed.

One day in July some years ago, I backpacked in to Little Rock Pond with my son, who was seven at the time, and we had planned to stay at the Lula Tye Shelter for a night. I was a little concerned about the weather, and even more about his enjoyment of the hike; I was hoping that he would take a positive imprint of backpacking. We started in a light rain, which didn't seem to bother him at all. As we approached the shelter we started noticing red efts. These are the immature phase of the eastern newt, a kind of salamander with bright orange with tiny yellow spots. Soon the ground was swarming with these "cute" creatures and my son became ecstatic, but we had to watch where we put our boots down.

When we reached the shelter and dropped our gear, he ran around through the woods collecting these easy-to-catch amphibians, placing them in a stockyard he made out of sticks and dirt. To this day he remembers the excitement of gently handling his temporary "pets" and has asked several times to go back there during a rain in summer.

The LT/AT arrives at the south end of Little Rock Pond where there is a trail junction. To the right is a camp area with tent platforms and the summer residence (a tent) of the GMC caretaker. Straight ahead, the LT/AT continues on its northerly course, skirting the east shore of the pond and passing a spring along the way. To the left, there is a path that joins the LT/AT at both ends of the pond, allowing for a circuit around it. The pathway on the west shore is quite narrow and rocky in places, however. Green Mountain, which towers over the western side of the pond, has its own trail, found at the north end of the pond, and offers a steep climb over ledges to a vista. The pond below and the mountains beyond are visible from that lookout. See Chapter 5, page 168, for more details on the Green Mountain Trail.

Ponds Accessible by High Clearance Vehicles: Little Pond, Branch Pond, Wallingford Pond

Little Pond

This small pond, located in the heart of snowmobile country, is remote and not too heavily frequented. A beaver lodge is located along its southwest shoreline, parts of which are bog-like. But it's not all that remote and peaceful. Motorized vehicles are able to get within 200 yards of it, which detracts considerably from the otherwise wilderness solitude. I've also seen people car camping along Forest Road 275 that leads to it. There are some very rough campsites near the shoreline, away from the road, but they don't look very comfortable. In spite of these problems, the pond is worth visiting, and hikers who are comfortable with bushwhacking can explore the more remote areas of shoreline away from the main trail. Little Pond is not recommended as a swimming area, but may be fine for fishing.

A large trailhead parking area for Little Pond is located on Route 9, 11.8 miles west of Wilmington, 9.4 miles east of Bennington, and 2.1 miles east of Prospect Mountain ski area.

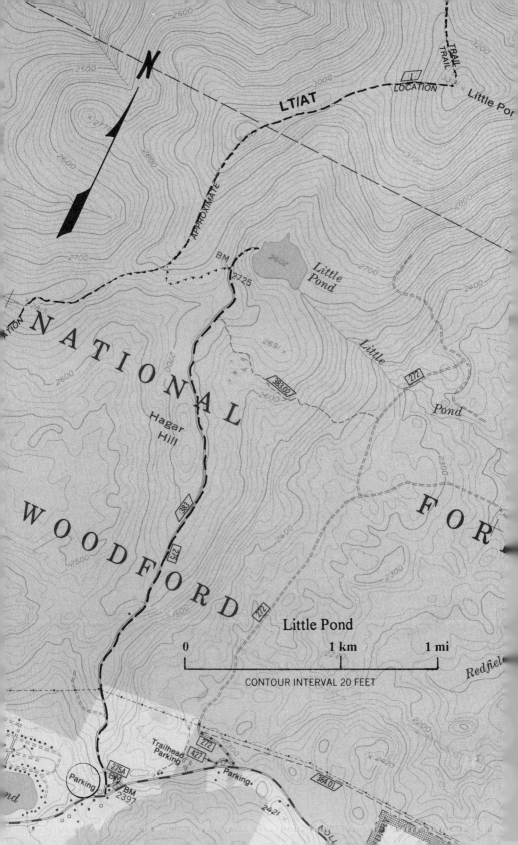

Little Pond

0   1 km   1 mi

CONTOUR INTERVAL 20 FEET

Although it would seem prudent to park here and walk the 2.5 miles to the pond, many people don't. On weekends in the summer or fall, you can expect to find people driving their SUVs all the way in, deepening the mud puddles and keeping the pathway wide for even more motor vehicles in the future. Still, hikers can make the best of this situation by hiking to the pond, then taking an old road to the LT/AT. From there, it is possible to hike to the Little Pond Lookout, or even beyond to the wooded summit of Little Pond Mountain.

From the trailhead parking on Route 9, begin hiking north on the rocky dirt road. As mentioned, the road has been beat up from use by light trucks and SUVs, so you can expect to navigate puddles. There are also some private residences being built in here and it is possible that the trail may be re-routed in the future. In about one-quarter mile, you'll pass an interesting sight, a rock painted up to look like a shark. The trail rises gradually in elevation and even offers some views at a powerline cut. The Haystack and Mount Snow range is the large mass to the east. Here the trail is on higher ground and passes through an open area which was once part of a camp. After about two miles of walking, there will be a junction with a trail on the right, which is an alternate snowmobile route. The next junction, which is a kind of turnaround that leads to a trail, is important. Here is where the road swings right down to the pond. Fortunately, most vehicles cannot go further than this junction. After a visit to the pond, return to this point.

From the turnaround area, find an old grassy lane that leads southwest. Take a compass bearing to be sure you are going SW and then follow this lightly used and overgrown lane through a large open area that is loaded with blackberries (ripe in September). When this lane reaches the woods on the other side of the opening, push through the vegetation and follow the continuation of the road west and north to a junction with the Long Trail/Appalachian Trail. A small cairn may mark this junction which you will need to remember to get back to your car. Turning left here will lead uphill and south for about a mile to the Porcupine Lookout, with views to the south and east. Turning right here will lead uphill and north for another mile to the Little Pond Lookout. From Little Pond to either lookout is probably about two miles or an hour of walking. Here you will find the serenity you might have missed at the pond itself.

Continuing another half mile north from Little Pond Lookout, you reach the summit of a peak that is labeled on the USGS maps as Little Pond Mountain, elevation 3,331 feet. This same name is given by the *Long Trail Guide* to the mountain where the lookout is located. From either of these Little Pond Mountains, retrace your steps to the junction with the connector lane, walk back to Little Pond, and then back to your car.

Branch Pond

[See Map #2 in Chapter 7, pages 158-159]

Forest Road 70 ends about a quarter mile from this secluded pond which lies just outside a wilderness boundary. This good-sized pond, about the same size as Bourn Pond, is popular with canoeists. It is bog-like in places and it has its own little island. There are a few campsites, accessible by canoe, along its shoreline. In order to put in a boat, it must be carried from the trailhead parking area down to the shoreline, which limits its use to lightweight canoes. My experiences with Branch Pond are minimal and mostly limited to glimpsing it from a side path off the Branch Pond Trail on the way to Bourn Pond. But from what I've seen, it's very beautiful and stays quite clean, no doubt due to the extra effort it takes to get a boat down into the water. (Extra effort tends to weed out the slobs.)

You can get to Branch Pond by driving north on Forest Road 70 which ends in about two miles at a parking area. Forest Road 70 is located off Arlington-West Wardsboro Road (Kelly Stand Road) 11.2 miles west of Route 100 and about 7 miles east of Route 7 (overpass). During the summer, you may see "dispersed campers" and their vehicles tucked into the few openings alongside Forest Road 70.

Less than one-half mile east of Forest Road 70, on the south side of Arlington-West Wardsboro Road, is tiny Beebe Pond. Like Branch Pond, this is also a pond used by canoeists, and it also requires some carrying from car to shoreline. It's a gem of a pond, and the walk down the path to the shoreline, though very short, is enjoyable.

Wallingford Pond

Wallingford Pond is in the White Rocks Recreation Area. It's almost like three ponds in one, with narrow channels connecting three larger bodies of water. The west lobe appears to get the most use, though I've not explored all of its shoreline. My experiences with this pond have been confined mostly to its south lobe. It's a very beautiful pond, with some beaver lodges, many birds, and a real sense of wilderness, that is until the sport utility vehicles start arriving with their cargo of boats and beer. It appears to me that most of the visitors to this pond never consider walking there. Drivers pass right by the trailhead parking near the end of Forest Road 20, then hang a left onto a narrow woods road that is apparently town road #39, drive up and down a hill, and hang another left onto the lane that leads down to the west lobe of the pond. This procedure keeps the mud puddles in good shape along the way. At the pond, some of these sport driving enthusiasts will attempt to get as far in as they can, even if this means getting stuck.

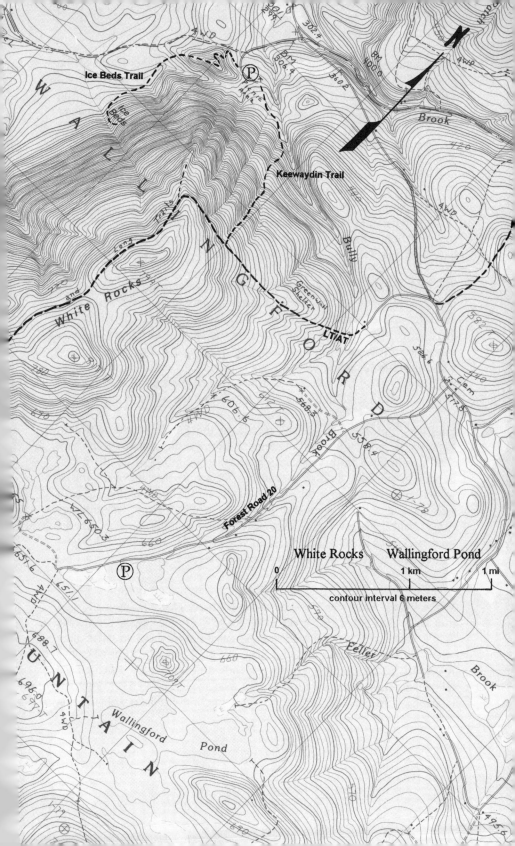

Ice Beds Trail

Keewaydin Trail

White Rocks

LT/AT

Brook

Bully

Greenwall
Shelter

Forest Road 20

White Rocks   Wallingford Pond

0   1 km   1 mi

contour interval 6 meters

Feller
Brook

Wallingford
Pond

One beautiful August night I was camping near the southern lobe of the pond with a friend and two children. The scene was completely peaceful and calm. We watched waterbirds on the pond and listened as the frog chorus got going. Darkness came, and with it, an even deeper and quieter peace. About an hour after dark, we suddenly heard a motor vehicle in the far distance, and it kept getting louder and louder. Then we heard another. The thought occurred to us that they might be coming our way, which was worrisome since we were camped near the woods road. Then, we heard sounds like a car was stuck in the mud. An engine was racing and stalling, racing and stalling. For the next two hours we were treated to a cacophony of these unnatural sounds, along with some indecipherable shouting. All of this was deeply disturbing, and it detracted considerably from what might have been a perfect experience of nature's beauty.

The next morning, we walked over to the area of the pond where the noise had come from, only to find two-foot-deep ruts, mud splattered everywhere, and piles of beer cans next to outrageously large fire rings. My friend was appalled by the environmental destruction to this wetland area and was concerned for the occupants of the beaver lodge nearby. I've been told that what was probably going on that night is called "mudding," a game played with two sport utility vehicles in which one deliberately gets stuck and "tries" to get out, and finally the other one pulls it out with a tow.

Following this incident, we stopped in at the Forest Service office in Manchester and filed a report. It seems that local residents have been using Wallingford Pond in this manner for years, making it hard for the Forest Service to suddenly enforce a change in behavior. In spite of all this, I would still recommend a hike out to this beautiful pond, preferably on a weekday and not on a summer or holiday weekend. Perhaps if more hikers cared about it and expressed their concern, things might change. As this guidebook goes to press, the Forest Service is developing a new policy that will formalize motorized access to Wallingford Pond.

You can get to Wallingford Pond from the same turnoff on Route 140 as White Rocks. From Wallingford, drive 2.1 miles east on Route 140 and turn right onto Sugar Hill Road. Don't make the immediate right into the White Rocks area, but continue straight ahead for another two miles, then turn right onto Wallingford Pond Road (Forest Road 20). In another two miles, just past a meadow, is a snowmobile trailhead parking area on the left. About one-quarter mile further, the road swings to the right. The trail to Wallingford Pond begins here. (Day-use parking is also possible in this area.)

Take the trail (more accurately, an SUV highway) and follow it uphill, staying with the main route and ignoring some trails that veer off on the right. After a descent, the lane arrives at a small clearing. To the left is the heavily-used area where vehicles go. Straight ahead and then to the left is the path to the more remote areas of the pond. (Note: Access to Wallingford Pond is in the process of being reviewed at the time of this writing. I've been told that the clearing just before the pond may become a parking area.)

Ponds For the Public

Grout Pond

Grout Pond is the centerpiece of a 1,600-acre tract that was once used by the Boy Scouts as a camp. It was called the Stratton Mountain Scout Reservation. The Forest Service acquired it in the late 1970s and it has since become a popular car-camping and boating area. It was named for the Grout family who once lived in the area. Grout Job and Grout Mills are the names of other places once associated with this family. The spring-fed Grout Pond is not small; it's one of the larger bodies of water in the Green Mountain National Forest. Grout Pond is fairly easy to get to, even in winter, when you can park on Arlington-West Wardsboro Road (Kelly Stand Road), which is plowed up to that point, and you can cross-country ski or snowshoe in. During the rest of the year, you can drive in with your car and unload your boat right by the water. There are campsites that you can drive right into, and some that you must paddle into.

Grout Pond is located south of Arlington-West Wardsboro Road, just 0.6 miles east of the LT/AT parking area for Stratton Mountain. From Route 100, drive 6.4 miles west. Near the end of the pavement, make a left onto the road to Grout Pond (Forest Road 262), which soon turns to dirt. It's less than a mile to the campsites and the caretaker zone of Grout Pond, and along the way you'll pass an opening that is designated as a "wildlife viewing area."

When you come to the camping area, the road will swing sharply left and descend to the pond. At this point, the resident caretaker may check up on what you are doing. Please give your respect to this person, as he is all that stands between order and chaos. A small donation is asked for using the area, a donation that goes to the local Forest Service District Office and may only be used for improvements at Grout Pond.

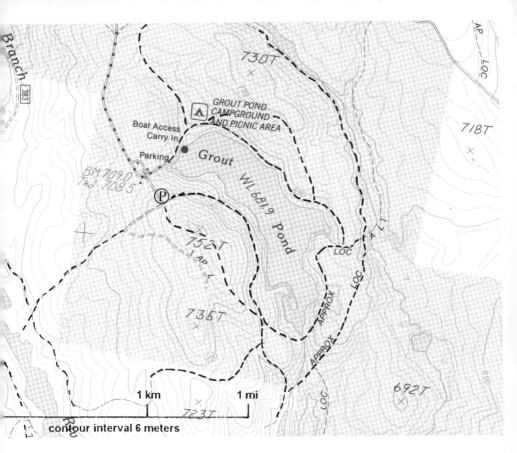

Hikers will find a few things to do at Grout Pond. There are a total of 12 miles of trail there -- trails that circle around the pond, plus several side trails. For the most part, these trails are lightly used and may offer a kind of solitude not found on the heavily-traveled LT/AT just to the north. The trails are generally marked with blue diamond blazes, to distinguish them from the orange markers used on snowmobile trails. In general, the Grout Pond trail system extends through the forest surrounding the pond, passing through some wetlands and meadows. The northern shoreline of Somerset Reservoir is accessible from this trail system. A map is available from the caretaker or from Forest Service headquarters in Manchester.

As mentioned, there are several camping possibilities at Grout Pond. Officially, there are nine campsites around the pond itself. Four of these are reachable only by canoe. There are three lean-tos that are available, as well. No reservations are needed, all sites are open to those who arrive first. Water is available from a hand pump, and outhouses are provided. Don't expect showers and hot water, however. Car-camping or canoe-camping at Grout Pond is fairly primitive.

140

One unfortunate use of some of the outlying woods roads around Grout Pond and Somerset Reservoir is called "mudding" or "bogging." I learned about this sport first hand while camping at Wallingford Pond one night, but I didn't know it had a name until I was informed of the terminology by Grout Pond's resident caretaker. He told me that the routine is based on the power-over-nature possibilities with today's sport utility vehicles. Two SUVs drive to a wet area on one of the forest roads, or just off one of these roads, and one proceeds to get stuck in the mud. After much wheel spinning, the other comes to its rescue with a tow cable and pulls it out. While this may sound like fun, it is very destructive to the environment, not to mention the awful sounds that are produced during the game.

It doesn't surprise me that this sport has caught on, given the anti-nature angle that is promoted by the vehicle manufacturers. The American public is constantly exposed to ads depicting SUV drivers as being on top of the world -- after they've churned up a path to the summit. SUV drivers are also portrayed as being better than geeky hikers who, god forbid, have to walk to get to the same place. Such is the world we live in today: Sell it anyway you can. ("Get out of my way, nature," says Marge Simpson as she plows through the woods in her new SUV.)

Hapgood Pond

The land around this pond was the first land to be acquired by the Forest Service in 1931 for the newly created Green Mountain National Forest. A mill that was located here cut logs for many years, powered by water from the pond. The campground may be of interest to those who wish to spend some time in the Green Mountains, and there's also a short trail that loops around both the pond and the campground that may be of interest to walkers. While Hapgood Pond is a part of the National Forest, it is operated by different concessionaires. User fees are charged.

Hapgood Pond is named for Marshall Hapgood who was a leader in the conservation movement. He was probably the town of Peru's most famous citizen, serving on the Vermont legislature and offering his land to the State to be permanent parkland. The Hapgood Pond Recreation Area opened in 1938, about the same time that Bromley Mountain became a scene for alpine skiing. Many of the structures that make up the recreation area were built by the Civilian Conservation Corps from 1936 to 1938.

From the junctions of Routes 30 and 11, just west of Bromley Mountain ski area, drive east on Route 11 for 3.5 miles and turn left to Peru. After only 0.3 mile, turn left again onto Hapgood Pond Road. (Note the John Stark monument ahead on the left). After 1 mile, bear right at the fork where the fire company building is. Hapgood Pond is just 0.7 miles ahead on the left.

141

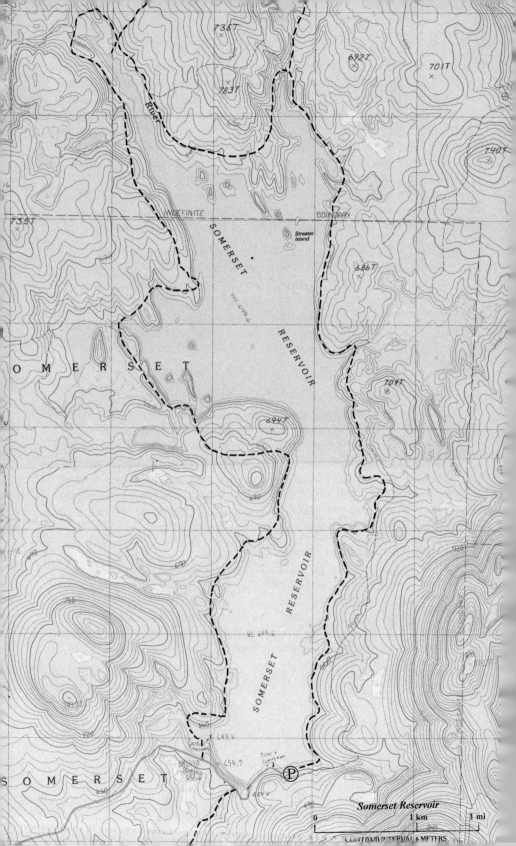

735T

692T

701T

723T

INDEFINITE

SOMERSET

Streeter
Island

BOUNDARY

735T

686T

RESERVOIR

S O M E R S E T

709T

694T

670

RESERVOIR

740T

920T

VL 649.6

SOMERSET

750

RESERVOIR

783.7T

720

649.4

Somerset Reservoir

BM 633.0

654.9

Picnic
Camping Area

632T

P

0   1 km   1 mi

660

654 V

670

CONTOUR INTERVAL 6 METERS

Reservoirs

Somerset Reservoir

Just northwest of Mount Snow and due south of Stratton Mountain is the 1,500+ acre Somerset Reservoir. It's a huge body of water, stretching over five miles from north to south and about a mile wide in the middle. From the huge dam at its southern end, Stratton Mountain stands boldly to the north. The steep north slope of Mount Snow is much closer, towering over the dam just to the southeast. Trails follow both the east and west shorelines. There's also the East Branch Trail that follows the river downstream from the reservoir which has some particularly scenic sections. It meets Forest Road 71 just above the point where the main branch of the Deerfield meets the East Branch.

Somerset Reservoir is the first in a series of water impoundments that stretch along the Deerfield River, which itself drains a good portion of the southern Green Mountains. The New England Power Company (NEPCo) was the agency in charge of this water path to Massachusetts, and the land around the various reservoirs is administered by them, not the Forest Service. Today, U.S. Generating has replaced NEPCo. Somerset Reservoir and Harriman Reservoir (described below) are important features within the overall boundaries of the Green Mountain National Forest and have much to offer hikers.

Prior to the building of the reservoir, loggers cut spruce in that area and sent the logs down the Deerfield River to the mills in Readsboro. These logging companies took out nearly all of the spruce, and they went for the hardwoods next. While spruce logs float well, hardwood doesn't. This, along with some other factors, led to the construction of logging railroads. Most of the intensive lumbering that was being done in southern Vermont was controlled by the Deerfield Lumber Company. In order to bring out the timber, they built narrow-gauge logging railroads well into the upper Deerfield Valley. By 1915 about forty miles of track had been laid and more than 25 logging camps operated in the forests. It was the peak of the harvesting of southern Vermont's virgin forests.

Meanwhile, the New England Power Company was formed in 1910. This corporation sought to acquire water rights along the Deerfield so they could build dams to generate electricity. They dammed the East Branch of the Deerfield River, creating the Somerset Reservoir. Besides generating electricity, it was used to float logs over to a rail line, which then carried them to mills and markets. Logging in the area was nearly over by 1930 because the resources of the forest had been used up. It must not have been a pretty sight.

Somerset Reservoir

Boat
Access

APPROXIMATE

LOCATION

SKI
LIFTS

Mount
Snow

East Branch Trail

G R E E N   M O U N T A I N

Branch

N A T I O N A L   F O R E S T

Flood Dam Trail

Deerfield

Searsburg Trail

Footbridge

Haystack
Mountain

0   1 km   1

CONTOUR INTERVAL 6 METERS

Just below the convergence of the two Deerfield branches is the Searsburg Reservoir. This small impoundment is located on the east side of Forest Road 71 just north of Route 9. From here, some of the water is diverted into a tube -- the big, black diversion tube that is visible from Route 9. The tube ends at a powerhouse and then the water rejoins the main flow and feeds the north end of the Harriman Reservoir.

The New England Power Company built several trails in the territory that was under their jurisdiction. These trails are generally not heavily used, are kept in reasonably good condition, and are for day-use only. Double-yellow markings seem to be the norm in this trail system. The East Shore and West Shore trails run along each side of Somerset Reservoir and are accessible from each side of the dam. Because the bridge is out at the north end of the reservoir, a circuit hike is not recommended. Both trails, however, offer many spectacular vistas over the water and out to peaks like Mount Snow, Stratton, and Glastenbury Mountain.

To reach the Somerset Reservoir, turn north onto Forest Road 71, 5.5 miles east of Wilmington. Drive another 6.3 miles on this dirt road and turn right after the road crosses over the Deerfield River. A sign here will note this turn. It's three miles, past an old school house and some residences, to the dam at the south end of the reservoir. The West Shore Trail begins here, near the western end of the dam. It utilizes old woods roads and has recently (1999) been cleared after years of neglect. The access road continues below the dam and ends at a picnic area on the southeast shore where the East Shore Trail begins. This footpath heads north along the shoreline, crossing streams and skirting coves. About three miles in (approximately 1.5 hours of hiking), a great shoreline view of Mount Snow and the Glastenbury range is found, about 0.1 mile past a brook crossing (where the trail changes direction from west to north). There's a boulder used (illegally) for a fireplace that marks the spot.

The East Branch Trail, which connects the Somerset Reservoir with Forest Road 71 just north of the Searsburg Reservoir, is also of interest to hikers. It's marked with double yellow blazes and leads for five miles through a series of meadows, ponds, and brook crossings, some on suspension bridges. The southern trailhead is located on the east side of Forest Road 71, 2.1 miles north of Route 9. Parking is very limited, but the trailhead is clearly marked by a sign just off the road. From here, the trail immediately crosses over the Deerfield River on a swinging suspension bridge and soon thereafter reaches a junction with the Flood Dam Trail on the left. (The unmaintained Flood Dam Trail heads north, following parts of an old railroad bed, to a pond about 2.3 miles away. This, and the remains of an old dam, are relics from the age of logging nearly a hundred years ago.)

145

Somerset Reservoir - view of Stratton Mountain

Somerset Reservoir - view of Mount Snow

From its junction with the Flood Dam Trail, the East Branch Trail turns sharply right and climbs over a low hill, descends, and crosses the East Branch of the Deerfield River on another suspension bridge. The trail turns left here and follows an old railroad bed for about a mile before turning away from the river and onto higher ground. Next, the trail traverses a mile or more of land managed by the Green Mountain National Forest, where blue markers designate the route. After leaving this section, the trail heads downhill, meets a junction with the East Branch Spur Trail (which leads down to the river) and ends at the Somerset Reservoir on the access road, just below the dam. There is ample parking here or at the nearby picnic area. Two features of the East Branch Trail are the beaver ponds passed along the way, and the views of the Mount Snow ridge.

I think the East Branch Trail would get more use if it were redesigned so as to offer several circular routes. Spotting cars at each end, or walking it both ways, are not appealing options for many people. One possibility is a strenuous hike combining the East Branch Trail and the Deerfield Ridge Trail between Haystack and Mount Snow, but this would involve some serious bushwhacking and boundary issues.

The Harriman Reservoir

The Harriman Reservoir, also known as Lake Whitingham, is Vermont's largest lake (over 2,000 acres) lying totally within its borders. It is fed by both the east and north branches of the Deerfield River, which merge in the lake and emerge below as the Deerfield River proper. Shaped like an undulating serpent, Harriman Reservoir is a popular recreation area and is used heavily by boaters, fishermen, picnickers, and swimmers (there's even a nude beach). A pseudo-steamship plies its waters during tourist season from a dock just off Route 9 west of Wilmington. On the east side of the reservoir, out of Green Mountain National Forest territory, are several public use areas. On its western shoreline is the Harriman Trail, an abandoned railroad grade that will appeal to hikers and cross-country skiers. The history of this rail-trail is quite interesting and is described in Chapter 2, page 23.

The 7.2-mile Harriman Trail is the relocated HT&W railroad bed (Hoosac Tunnel and Wilmington, a.k.a. "Hoot Toot & Whistle"). It can be walked from end to end as a rail-trail because there are convenient parking areas at both the north and south trailheads. This route is also a part of the Catamont Trail, a 280-mile cross-country ski trail marked with blue diamond/catprint tags, which will someday span the length of Vermont.

147

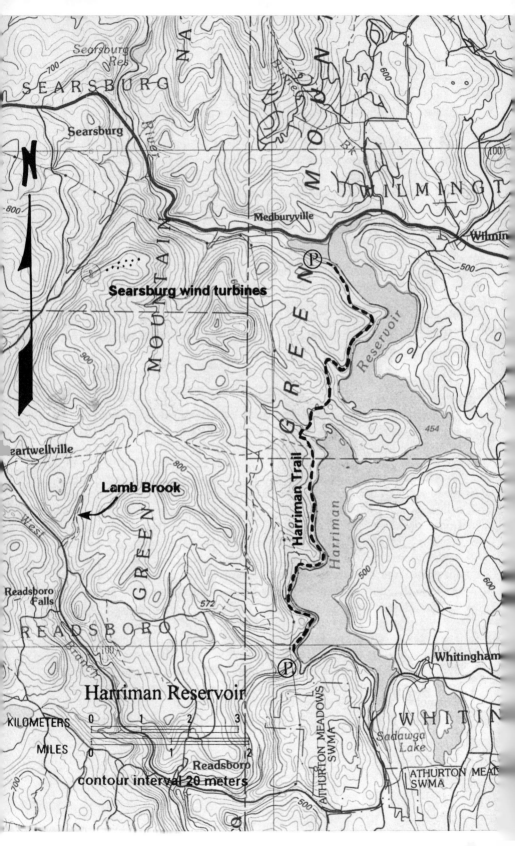

The entire Harriman Trail is within the overall boundaries of the Green Mountain National Forest. I found this trail to be bursting with wildflowers in the month of May. The "edge" created by the trail is filled with spring beauties, trout lilies, trillium, and dutchman's breeches.

There are two trailheads for the Harriman Trail, north and south. The northern one is located at the NEPCo (now U.S. Generating) Mountain Mills West picnic area. Take Route 9 west from Wilmington for 2.8 miles, turn left onto Woods Road, cross the bridge (which is next to an old bridge), and then turn left again. The picnic area is a mile ahead. The southern trailhead, which is more remote and passes over the dam, is just off Route 100 between Whitingham and Readsboro. From Wilmington center, travel east on Route 9 to Route 100 South. Then drive seven miles to Jacksonville. At Jacksonville turn right twice, staying on Route 100. Four miles ahead is Whitingham and Brown's General Store, and another mile on Route 100 brings you to Harriman Road. Turn right here and drive 1.8 miles to a hairpin turn and, immediately after that, a parking area that is located in front of a gate to the Harriman Dam.

If you are hiking the Harriman Trail from its south end, be sure to take a good look at the Glory Hole drain. This unique way of handling excess water is a marvel of engineering. Water spilling over the edge of the Glory Hole drops 170 feet to the bottom of the dam. The cone itself is 160 feet wide and tapers to 22 feet at its base. The spillway actually looks like a morning glory flower during periods of high water when water pours over its lip. Most of the year, however, there is not enough water to create that kind of effect. When water levels are high, however, the Glory Hole allows the level of the reservoir to be varied by the placement of boards along the rim of the spillway.

The Harriman Trail is not heavily used, so if you walk early in the day, on weekdays, or off-season, you may be alone. The reservoir itself, however, is heavily used by boaters during the summer and you may expect to hear the sounds of motorized boats from time to time. The only markers you will see on this trail are the occasional double yellow blazes of the power company, and the blue tags of the Catamount Trail. Obviously, an end-to-end hike would require parking cars at each trailhead. If you have only one car, consider hiking the Harriman Trail from the southern trailhead. This will give you a good feel for the trail, plus a look at the dam. The parking situation, at least during weekends, is generally better there also. The northern trailhead, so close to Wilmington, is often filled with picnickers and fishing enthusiasts.

Harriman Reservoir -- west shoreline

Hikers beginning at the southern trailhead should leave the parking area in the following way -- if the main gate is closed. About 150 feet left of the main gate, and between a large white birch and a maple tree, is an unusual opening that allows an individual, but not a motorized vehicle, access to the dam. Pass through the gate and follow the paved path beneath the dam. At a hairpin turn near power lines at the end of the dam, turn right (still on the pavement) and walk to the top of the dam, now facing the reservoir. Continue straight ahead onto the unpaved railroad bed that follows the western shore of the reservoir. You are now on the Harriman Trail. A blue Catamont Ski Trail tag may be posted in this area.

The trail passes through a narrow rock cut, then further on descends to a brook and a four-way junction. A right turn here leads past a stone wall and a secluded picnic table and down to the reservoir. Continuing on the Harriman Trail for another mile and a half takes you to a bridge over Graves Brook. The original rail bed must have been on some kind of trestle at this point because the existing path descends abruptly to the brook, then climbs right back up to its previous level. The bridge over Graves Brook, which is very near the shoreline, and near the halfway point of the trail, is a good place to stop, climb out over the rocks to the reservoir, and take in the scenery. It's also a good place to turn around and head back to the dam. (The total mileage to this point is about 3.5 miles.)

If you choose to continue on, the next mile of the Harriman Trail is filled with the remains of old railroad ties and spikes, and swings gradually to the west. It passes some rock walls and crosses an old stagecoach road, constructed in the 1760s, that leads west to Heartwellville. This road, used by snowmobiles, passes through the heart of the Lamb Brook area on its way to Route 8. A short distance further and the Harriman Trail leaves the railbed and descends on a footpath to cross Wilder Brook on a hiker's bridge. After climbing back up to the level of the railroad grade, the footpath meets the railroad bed again and turns left. A turn to the right here leads in about 200 feet to the edge of the ravine over Wilder Brook, cascading below. A trestle once spanned this deep ravine.

The last three miles of the Harriman Trail follow the old railroad bed, passing through several rock cuts, the first quite dramatic. A staging area for logging and a somewhat bizarre private camp are passed on the way to the Mountain Mills West picnic area where the northern trailhead is located. This section of the trail receives more vehicle use than the first section and is maintained to some extent.

Harriman Dam area

151

Chapter 7

Day-hiking and Backpacking

For those who simply want to be directed to the classic day-hikes of the Green Mountain National Forest, here's a short list. All of these hikes are very popular and hikers should expect to encounter many others on the trail, as well as at the parking lot. It would be best to hike these areas during low use periods, such as weekdays and off-season.

Classic Day-Hikes   See Page

Haystack Mountain	Chapter 5	87
Harmon Hill	Chapter 5	113
Stratton Mountain	Chapter 5	92
Stratton Pond	Chapter 6	123
Lye Brook and the waterfall	Chapter 4	76
Prospect Rock	Chapter 4	80
Bromley Mountain	Chapter 5	99
Baker Peak	Chapter 5	119
Little Rock Pond	Chapter 6	131
White Rocks and Ice Beds	Chapter 5	121

Backpacking

The greatest hiking trail in the Green Mountain National Forest is, of course, the Long Trail. I've been hiking along this trail for years and have walked nearly all of it, but a few short pieces here and there have eluded me because it is an end-to-end trail. If you have only one car, a 10-mile section of the Long Trail, which is half of an official *Long Trail Guide* section, requires a 20-mile day hike, something I don't often have time for. In other words, to hike a typical 20-mile section of the Long Trail, utilizing one car, requires hiking 40 miles round-trip. Much of the time I hike by myself, so spotting cars at each end of a hike is impossible.

There's also the fact that energy conservation should be considered. Two cars burns more gas, and there is no public transportation. What has worked better for me is to do long circular hikes, good for strenuous day-hiking or overnight backpacking.

contour interval 20 meters

Hikers of all abilities should take the hikes described below seriously. Be sure to plan your hike carefully and let others know where you are going. Sign in at all trail registers and sign out when you leave the area. If you are backpacking, you should be prepared to pay a camping fee to the many Green Mountain Club caretakers who keep an eye on the natural areas that make our visits to the Green Mountain National Forest so interesting and satisfying. The basic rules of the trail are: Take out whatever you bring in, be respectful of nature and other trail users, and don't push yourself beyond your capacity. The hiking guidelines found in the Introduction may also be helpful for trip preparation.

Glastenbury Mountain Loop
[See Map #1, facing page]

Only those in excellent condition with plenty of trail experience should attempt this 22-mile hike with a vertical rise of 3,600 feet. It's too long for a day-hike, but it makes an excellent two-or-three-day backpack. It's also fairly popular and I've run across many people who have hiked the loop. In fact, the April '96 issue of *Outside Magazine* listed this hike as Vermont's best. Nearly all of the route is on foot-trails, there are two shelters along the way, and the views from the summit of Glastenbury give a real sense of how vast this section of the Green Mountain National Forest really is. There is an additional two-mile road walk necessary to complete the loop. A detailed description of this hike is found in *50 Hikes in Vermont* by the Green Mountain Club.

The trailhead for this hike is the Long Trail/Appalachian Trail parking area on the north side of Route 9, just over five miles east of Bennington. From this large parking lot, cross the bridge over City Stream and hike north and uphill, following the white markers of the LT/AT. At 1.6 miles, a trail on the right leads to the Melville Nauheim Shelter. Past the shelter, the LT/AT climbs to a power line cut that offers some views, and heads northward to Glastenbury Mountain, some eight miles distant. Along the way are several lookouts.

Just south of the round, wooded summit of Glastenbury Mountain is the Goddard Shelter, an open log shelter with views to the south. This shelter, along with the few tent sites nearby, is near the half-way point in the hike. In front of the shelter, down below in the rough clearing, is the vague beginning of the West Ridge Trail, your return route. The actual summit of the mountain, where there is an observation tower, is 0.3 miles north of the shelter on the LT/AT.

155

To return to the start of this loop, follow the sporadic blue markers of the West Ridge Trail down from Glastenbury Mountain. The route follows several logging roads, skirts the semi-boreal forest of an unnamed summit (referred to in this guidebook as West Ridge Mountain), then continues along a rocky path to the somewhat open summit of Bald Mountain. At a junction marked with signs, turn left onto the Bald Mountain Trail and head downhill to the east and Woodford Hollow. Keep track of the marked route which follows several woods roads. It's about two miles down to the road where there is a large concrete water tank. Turn right here and walk about a mile to Route 9. Turn left and walk the last mile to your car.

Stratton Mountain and Stratton Pond Loop
[See Map #2, pages 158-159]

This very popular loop hike takes in the highest summit in the southern Green Mountains, one of its most remote ponds, and plenty of wild forest in between. The total distance is about 12 miles (including a one-mile road walk) with a total elevation gain of about 2,000 feet. The are good camping possibilities at Stratton Pond, but you should expect to pay a fee to the GMC caretaker between Memorial Day and Columbus Day. It's worth it, however, because the place is kept clean. If possible, avoid a weekend hike to this over-used area. On weekdays you have a much better chance of spotting wildlife, finding a campsite, and enjoying the natural qualities of the area.

The hike begins off Arlington-West Wardsboro Road (Kelly Stand Road) at the Long Trail/Appalachian Trail parking area seven miles west of Route 100. (You actually have two choices as starting points for this hike. The LT/AT parking area just noted, or the Stratton Pond parking area a mile further west. It depends on whether or not you want to begin òr end your hike with a road walk -- or whether one of the lots is full of cars. From the LT/AT parking area, follow the white markers away from the road and into a sometimes wet and boggy woods. The trail remains more or less level for about a mile, crosses a forest road/snowmobile corridor, and then begins to climb the north side of Stratton Mountain. The north summit of Stratton is only skirted by the trail which is now near the edge of the boreal forest. The last mile continues the steady climb and passes two lookouts on the way. The summit is wooded, but there is a firetower that offers spectacular 360-degree views. For those that like to keep their feet on the ground, views are possible from the ski slopes a half mile north on the unmarked trail.

From Stratton's summit, the LT/AT descends the mountain, crosses a stream and the forest road/snowmobile corridor, and then enters a low wet area surrounded by beaver ponds and meadows. A gradual climb to a low ridge brings the trail to a junction with the Stratton Pond Trail. Turn right here and walk down to the pond at a small clearing. The GMC caretaker lives here and s/he will explain your camping options. A trail encircles the pond allowing access to the North Shore Tenting Area and other tenting areas A new shelter, located away from the pond (off the Stratton Pond Trail) is being constructed (1999) by the Worcester, Massachusetts, Section of the GMC.

The return leg of the hike is via the Stratton Pond Trail, which meets the LT/AT just south of and above the pond. This 3.7-mile footpath rises and falls, gradually climbing a few hundred feet and then descending to Arlington-West Wardsboro Road. If you parked here at the Stratton Pond Trail parking area, your car is just to your right. If you parked at the LT/AT lot, turn left and walk the mile back to it on the road.

Once at Stratton Pond, a backpacking trip can be extended by utilizing a loop formed by the LT/AT north of the pond, the Branch Pond Trail, and the Lye Brook Trail. This loop, which is just under ten miles in length, passes two shelters along the way. For more information, see Chapter 4, page 73, the Lye Brook Wilderness, and the description below.

At the Vondell Shelter (removed in 1999)

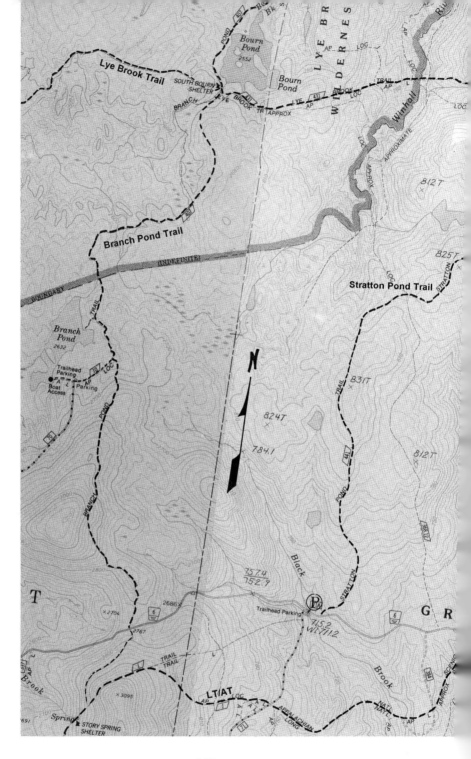

Lye Brook Trail

SOUTH BOURN SHELTER

Bourn Pond 2552

Bourn Pond

L Y E   B R   W I L D E R N E S

BRANCH

LYE BROOK TR APPROX

LYE   41   BROOK

TRAIL

Winhall

R I U

APPROXIMATE

LOG

812 T

Branch Pond Trail

UNDEFINED

BOUNDARY

825 T

Stratton Pond Trail

STRATTON

TRAIL

Branch Pond 2632

Trailhead Parking

LOG

831 T

AP Parking

Boat Access

824 T

784.1

POND

44 T

812 T

70

BRANCH

POND

STRATTON

Black

757.4
752.9

T

×2704

6

2686×

Trailhead Parking

P

G   R

6

2767

752
W 711.2

Brook

Brook

TRAIL

TRAIL

×3095

LT/AT

LOC

APPALACHIAN   LONG

NAT'L
NAT'L

SCENIC

Spring

2691

STORY SPRING SHELTER

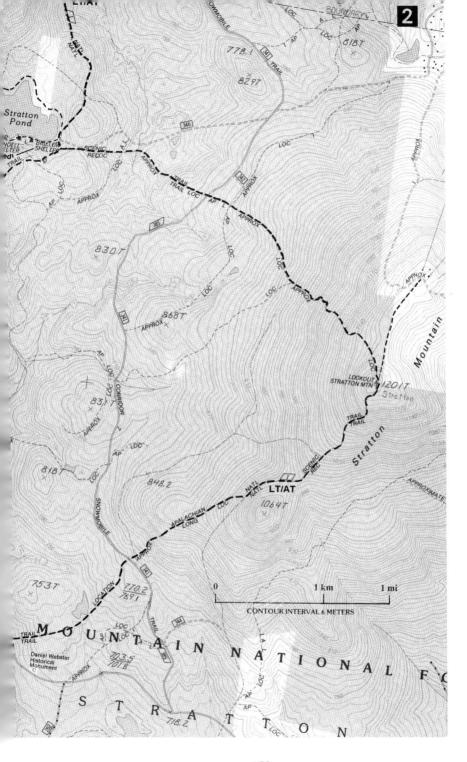

Lye Brook to Prospect Rock Loop
[See Map #2 in this Chapter, pages 158-159
and Lye Brook Map in Chapter 4, pages 74-75]

The huge Lye Brook Wilderness area (15,000+ acres) is penetrated by two footpaths, the Lye Brook Trail and the Branch Pond Trail. A wonderful loop hike of about 15.5 miles, mostly through this wilderness, is possible using a section of the LT/AT, the dirt Rootville Road, and a paved road walk of just over two miles. There are good camping possibilities at two points along the way, Bourn Pond and the William B. Douglass Shelter, and there's also a great vista from Prospect Rock.

Park your car at the trailhead for the Lye Brook Trail which is near Manchester. From Routes 11 & 30, about 0.5 mile east of Route 7 (exit 4), turn south onto East Manchester Road. Follow this road, which will swing to the right, for just over a mile and turn left onto Glenn Road. Keep to the right at a fork and drive another 0.4 mile to the circular trailhead parking area.

The hike begins on the Lye Brook Trail which is marked with blue blazes and generally follows Lye Brook into the wilderness. Most of the route utilizes an old railroad bed (see Chapter 4, page 76). Just under two miles into the hike, a right turn at a junction leads to a high waterfall, said to be Vermont's highest. (If you take this detour, which is well worth it, it will add another mile to your hike.) From this junction, the Lye Brook Trail continues uphill, then gradually levels off as the high Green Mountain plateau is attained. The trail gets wilder. Meadows, beaver ponds, and old lumber clearings are passed on the way to Bourn Pond.

The Lye Brook Trail arrives at Bourn Pond in back of the Bourn Pond Shelter. Since this shelter and the other nearby campsites are near the halfway point of the hike, they make a good choice for an overnight stay. The shelter is located at a nexus of trails which could be confusing.

The Lye Brook Trail continues on to Stratton Pond, but to complete the loop you must now follow the Branch Pond Trail along the west shore of Bourn Pond and north to its junction with the LT/AT. The Branch Pond Trail is found in front of and below the shelter and it follows the shoreline of the pond to its northern end. From there it continues north, routed on another old rail line.

160

About 3.5 miles north from Bourn Pond, the Branch Pond Trail arrives at the William B. Douglass Shelter, another overnight option for a two-day trip. Hiking another half mile from the shelter, the Branch Pond Trail ends at a junction with the LT/AT. Turn left here and follow the LT/AT along old Rootville Road to Prospect Rock, just under a mile ahead. Here, to the left of the trail, is a wonderful view of Downer Glenn (which lies within the Lye Brook Wilderness), the town of Manchester, and massive Mount Equinox behind it.

From Prospect Rock, leave the LT/AT and continue downhill on old Rootville Road. (The LT/AT turns off the road across from Prospect Rock and heads north on a footpath.) Rootville Road descends steadily, passes a small glen with water shooting over tilted rock beds, and emerges near a residence and a water tank. Here is where the two-mile road walk begins. Continue down Rootville Road for just over a half mile, turn left onto East Manchester Road and walk a mile to Glenn Road. Turn left here, keep right and walk back to your car at the trailhead.

Descending on Rootville Road

Styles Peak/Peru Peak/Griffith Lake Loop
[See Map #3, page 163]

This eleven-mile hike enters the Peru Peak Wilderness on the Long Trail/ Appalachian Trail and returns following the wilderness boundaries via a snowmobile corridor and two Forest Service Roads. Although hiking on Forest Service Roads isn't particularly inviting, there is an outstanding vista from one of them on the return trip. Making this hike an overnight is also possible with a Long Trail shelter and a camping area near Griffith Lake at about the halfway point.

The hike starts at the LT/AT parking area in Mad Tom Notch. From Routes 11 & 30 at Peru (about two miles east of Bromley ski area), turn north and then keep left onto Hapgood Pond Road. In one mile the road will fork again, where you will bear left. In 0.8 miles, turn left onto Mad Tom Notch Road, which is also Forest Road 21. The LT/AT parking area is 2.2 miles ahead and uphill, on the left side of the road.

Begin hiking north on the LT/AT, heading towards Styles Peak. This is the steepest climb of the loop -- it's a mile long and nearly 1,000 feet up to the summit of Styles Peak. A rock outcrop offers a view out to the east and south. The trail continues north along a high ridge in a boreal forest. After another mile and a half, Peru Peak is reached, which has a more limited overlook. A descent from the summit leads to the Peru Peak Shelter, located near a rushing stream. From the shelter, the LT/AT continues heading north, now through wet areas, reaching Griffith Lake, and further, a tenting area. You can expect to meet GMC caretakers at both the shelter and the lake where campers are asked to pay a fee.

Continue around Griffith Lake passing a junction with the Old Job Trail, which is a snowmobile trail. Where the LT/AT turns north (meeting the Lake Trail not far from the lake), keep to the left and follow the snowmobile trail (Corridor 7) alongside the lake. You should now be heading south, with the lake to your left. A small clearing is the former site of Silas Griffith's lake house (see Chapter 6, page 128). Continue north, following the snowmobile corridor which is an old road bed that may be muddy in places. About two miles from the lake, you will arrive at the end of Forest Road 58 where there is a small parking area. This is "Porky Point," so named because many cars parked overnight there have had important rubber hoses destroyed by roving, nocturnal porcupines.

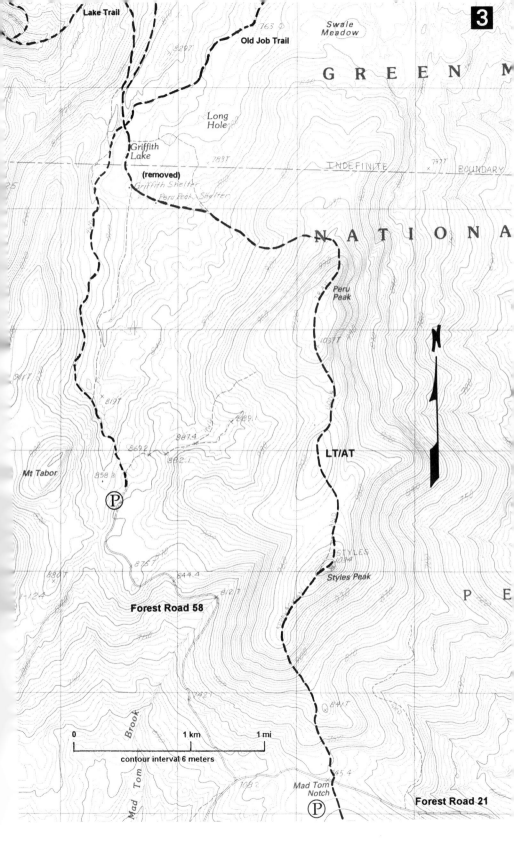

3

Lake Trail

Old Job Trail

Swale
Meadow

G R E E N   M

Long
Hole

Griffith
Lake

(removed)

Griffith Shelter

Peru Peak Shelter

INDEFINITE   BOUNDARY

N A T I O N A

Peru
Peak

LT/AT

Mt Tabor

P

STYLES

Styles Peak

P E

Forest Road 58

Brook

0   1 km   1 mi

contour interval 6 meters

Mad Tom

Mad Tom
Notch

P

Forest Road 21

From Porky Point, follow Forest Road 58 for about three miles. While the walk is fairly level, and fairly boring for the most part, you will pass by a spectacular view down the eastern flanks of the Green Mountains into the Valley of Vermont. After a descent, the road will meet Forest Road 21. Turn left here and walk uphill to the LT/AT parking area about a half mile ahead.

Trout Lilies on Peru Peak

Old Job/Griffith Lake/Baker Peak Loop
[See Map #4, page 166]

This strenuous 14+ mile hike with an elevation gain of about 1,400 feet begins at the LT/AT parking area on Forest Road 10 near Big Branch. The hike crests at the bare outcrop on Baker Peak, drops down to remote Griffith Lake, and passes through what is left of an old logging community at Old Job. Along the way are three shelters and one tenting area. The hike can be reduced to about 11 miles by starting at the end of Forest Road 30. Much of the hike travels through the Big Branch Wilderness, and some of it follows a section of the Old Job Trail which is really snowmobile Corridor 7.

Backpackers should park at one of the LT/AT parking areas at Big Branch. From Route 7, at the crossroads between Danby and Mount Tabor (see directions to Little Rock Pond or Green Mountain, page 121), turn east on Brooklyn Road. Following signs to Mount Tabor, cross the railroad tracks, and enter the National Forest. Two parking areas are located on the south side of Forest Road 10, at 3.1 and 3.3 miles east of Route 7. The first lot is paved and larger, built to accommodate the many who hike to Little Rock Pond. The second area is along the side of the road where signs direct you to points south on the LT/AT.

From the parking area, follow the white markers of the LT/AT east and downhill towards Big Branch Brook. A shelter is located here, near the brook. After following the brook for a short distance, the LT/AT crosses it on a suspension bridge. Just ahead of this crossing is a junction with the Old Job Trail, which will be your return route (unless you decide to do the hike in reverse). The trail now turns south and climbs gradually toward Baker Peak, about 3.5 miles away. Halfway there is a side trail leading to the second shelter on the hike, the Lost Pond Shelter.

Five miles from the start of the hike is Baker Peak, a bare strip of ledge offering great views out to Dorset Mountain and beyond. Staying on the LT/AT, a gradual descent followed by a level stretch through a wet area will bring you to Griffith Lake at a junction with the Old Job Trail, a.k.a. snowmobile Corridor 7. If you follow the LT/AT south along the east shore of the lake, you'll come to the Griffith Lake Tenting Area. A half mile further south leads to the Peru Peak Shelter. You can expect to pay a fee for camping at either place between Memorial Day and Columbus Day as a GMC caretaker will, no doubt, be on duty. If you are backpacking, these areas would be good choices to spend the night because they are located at about the half way point of the hike. Camping is not allowed within 200 feet of the lake except where allowed by the GMC caretaker.

The Great Sawdust Pile

To return to your starting point, take the occasionally blue-blazed Old Job Trail north from Griffith Lake. Follow its sometimes muddy route carefully as it intersects a few other woods roads. As mentioned, this logging road is also snowmobile Corridor 7, the winter superhighway for the Vermont Association of Snow Travelers (VAST).

The trail, which is more like a cleaned-up woods road, follows Lake Brook, the drainage of Griffith Lake, until it reaches the terminus of Forest Road 30. Beyond this road, the Old Job Trail becomes more like a footpath. A mile north of the road, the Old Job Shelter is reached, located amongst old apple trees. The trail then crosses Lake Brook on another suspension bridge, passes an ancient mound of sawdust (nothing can grow on it) and winds its way through an abandoned apple orchard. All of this is what remains of Old Job, a logging community that packed up and left when the wood ran out.

167

At the end of the orchard, the Old Job Trail follows Lake Brook along a level railroad grade and soon arrives at its junction with the LT/AT. The bridge over Big Branch is just ahead on the LT/AT and the parking area is another 1.2 miles beyond that.

Day-hikers who wish to shorten the loop can start the hike at the end of Forest Road 30. From Route 7 in Danby, drive 6.7 miles east on Forest Road 10. Turn right (south) onto Forest Road 30 and drive another 2.3 miles to its end at the Old Job Trail and Lake Brook. Parking is alongside the road. The loop using the Old Job Trail and the LT/AT could be done in either direction, though making a right turn and heading toward Old Job first will leave you with a fast walk back from Griffith Lake.

Little Rock Pond/Green Mountain Loop
[See Map #5, page 169]

The LT/AT parking area on Forest Road 10 detailed above is also a starting point for a circular hike of about seven miles, this one north of the road. The total elevation gain on the hike is about 1,300 feet. Two outstanding features, Little Rock Pond and the ledges on Green Mountain, plus several overnight camping possibilities, draw many hikers to the area. Weekends in summer and early fall can be crowded, though most people use only the LT/AT to reach these destinations. The Green Mountain Trail receives less use.

The starting point for this hike is the LT/AT parking area on Forest Road 10, 3.1 miles from Route 7 (see directions for Little Rock Pond or Green Mountain, page 121). From the parking area, walk back (west) down Forest Road 10 for about 100 yards to the trailhead for the Green Mountain Trail Connector and follow this downhill, parallel to the road, to a junction with a path that leads down to the Big Branch Picnic Area. Don't take this path, instead stay with the blue blazes of the Green Mountain Trail which will begin to climb and swing sharply to the right. A limited vista, looking to the west, is passed at this point.

The trail, now heading north and gradually climbing, and passing under some very large trees, uses an old woods road for part of its route. After roughly 3.5 miles, the trail finally crests the ridge of Green Mountain. The footing is rockier here and several excellent vistas are found to the right of the trail. (You may have to do a little exploring to find the best ones.) For the next mile the trail descends the mountain over exposed ledges, reaching the Little Rock Pond Trail, which allows for a circular walk around the pond. Turn left here and follow the path over the pond's outlet to a junction with the LT/AT.

168

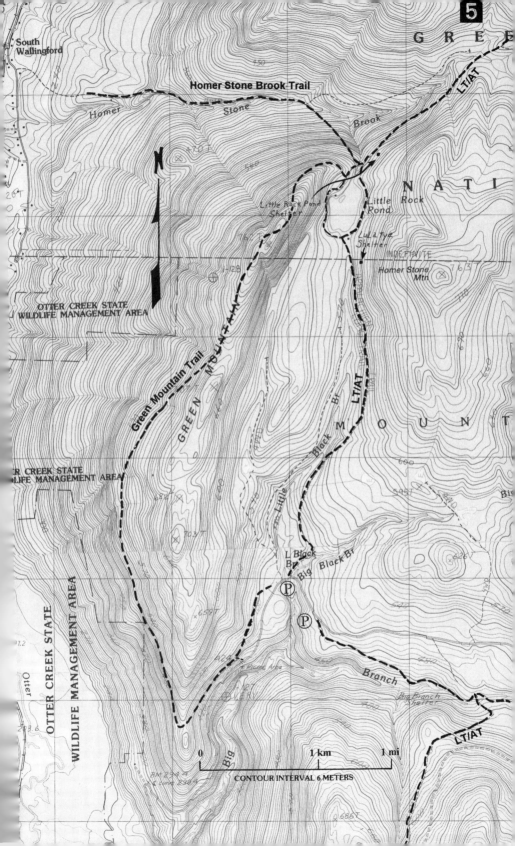

South
Wallingford

G R E E

Homer Stone Brook Trail

Homer   Stone   Brook

LT/AT

N A T I

N

Little Rock Pond
Shelter

Little Rock
Pond

Lula Tye
Shelter

INDEFINITE

Homer Stone
Mtn

OTTER CREEK STATE
WILDLIFE MANAGEMENT AREA

Green Mountain Trail

G R E E N   M O U N T A I N

LT/AT

CREEK STATE
LIFE MANAGEMENT AREA

Black Br

Little

M O U N T

L Black
Br

Big Black Br

P

P

OTTER CREEK STATE

WILDLIFE MANAGEMENT AREA

Branch

Big Branch
Shelter

LT/AT

Otter

BM 294.4

Big

0   1 km   1 mi

CONTOUR INTERVAL 6 METERS

The Ledges of Green Mountain

Turn right (south) on the LT/AT and follow it along the eastern shore of the pond. (A left turn at this junction leads to the Little Rock Pond Shelter, which was formerly located on the pond's island.) If you have backpacked in, you have several camping options. There are two shelters, the just mentioned Little Rock Pond Shelter which is north of the pond, and the Lula Tye Shelter south of it. There are some tent sites near the north end of the pond and some tent platforms near the south end. During hiking season a GMC caretaker will be living at one of the tent platforms, doing crowd-control work and collecting camping fees.

To complete the loop and return to your car, follow the white blazes of the LT/AT south. The Lula Tye Shelter will be uphill to your left about a quarter mile south of the pond. Another 1.7 miles on flat terrain will lead to Forest Road 10. This section of the hike receives probably ten times as much traffic as the Green Mountain Trail.

References

Bucholt, Margaret, ed. *An Insider's Guide to Southern Vermont.* New York: Penguin Books. 1991.

Curtis, Jane and Will, and Frank Lieberman. *Green Mountain Adventure: Vermont's Long Trail.* Montpelier, VT: The Green Mountain Club. 1985.

Johnson, Charles W. *The Nature of Vermont.* Hanover, NH: The University Press of New England. 1980.

Jorgensen, Neil. *A Guide to New England's Landscape.* Chester, CT: Pequot Press. 1977.

Lee, W. Storrs. *The Green Mountains of Vermont.* NY: Henry Holt. 1955.

Raymo, Chet and Maureen E. Raymo. *Written in Stone.* Chester, CT: The Globe Pequot Press. 1989.

Rood, Ronald. "Green Mountain National Forest: 50 Years in Vermont." Supplement to *Sunday Rutland Herald & Sunday Times Argus,* 6/20/1982.

Swift, Esther Munroe. *Vermont Place Names: Footprints of History.* Brattleboro, VT: The Stephen Greene Press. 1977.

WPA writers. *Vermont: A Guide to the Green Mountain State.* Boston: Houghton Mifflin Company. 1937.

Recommended Reading

The Audubon Society Nature Guides. Eastern Forests. New York: Chanticleer Press. 1992.

The Green Mountain Club. *Day Hiker's Guide to Vermont.* Waterbury Center, VT. 1989.

---. *Fifty Hikes in Vermont.* Woodstock, VT: Backcountry Pubs. 1997.

---. *Long Trail Guide.* Waterbury Center, VT: 1996.

Mikolas, Mark. *Nature Walks in Southern Vermont.* Boston, MA: Appalachian Mountain Club Books. 1995.

Nash, Roderick. *Wilderness and the American Mind.* New Haven, CT: Yale University Press. 1967, 1973.

Pletcher, Larry. *Hiking Vermont.* Helena, MT: Falcon Publishing. 1996.

Waterman, Laura and Guy. *Wilderness Ethics.* Woodstock, VT: The Countryman Press. 1992.

Important Contact Information

Green Mountain National Forest:

Manchester Ranger District
District Ranger, USDA Forest Service
2538 Depot Street
Manchester Center, VT 05255-9419
Fax: 802/362-1251
Phone: 802/362-2307
TTY: 802/362-2307

Forest Supervisor
231 North Main Street
Rutland, VT 05701-2417
Phone: 802/747-6700
Fax: 802/747-6766
TTY: 802/747-6765
Website: *www.fs.fed.us./r9/gmfl*
Email: (names) */r9_gmfl2fs.fed.us*

The Green Mountain Club:

The Green Mountain Club
4711 Waterbury-Stowe Road
Waterbury Center, VT 05677
Phone: 802/244-7037
Fax: 802/244-5867
E-mail: *gmc@sover.net*
Website: *www.greenmountainclub.org*

Forest Watch

Forest Watch
10 Langdon St.
Montpelier, VT 05602
Phone: 802/223-3216
Website: *www.forestwatch.org*

Map Index

General Index

Other Products from
New England Cartographics

Maps

Holyoke Range State Park (Eastern Section)	$3.95
Holyoke Range/Skinner State Park (Western)	$3.95
Mt. Greylock Reservation Trail Map	$3.95
Mt. Toby Reservation Trail Map	$3.95
Mt. Tom Reservation Trail Map	$3.95
Mt. Wachusett and Leominster State Forest Trail Map	$3.95
Western Massachusetts Trail Map Pack (all 6 above)	$15.95
Quabbin Reservation Guide	$4.95
Quabbin Reservation Guide (waterproof version)	$5.95
New England Trails (general locator map)	$2.95
Grand Monadnock Trail Map	$3.95
Connecticut River Map (in Massachusetts)	$5.95

Books

Guide to the Metacomet-Monadnock Trail	$8.95
Hiking the Pioneer Valley	$10.95
Skiing the Pioneer Valley	$10.95
Bicycling the Pioneer Valley	$10.95
Hiking the Monadnock Region	$12.95
High Peaks of the Northeast	$12.95
Great Rail Trails of the Northeast	$14.95
Golfing in New England	$16.95
24 Great Rail Trails of New Jersey	$16.95
Steep Creeks of New England	$14.95
Hiking Green Mountain National Forest, So. Section	$14.95

Subtotal _____

Please include postage/handling:
$0.75 for the first single map and $0.25 for each additional map;
$1.50 for the Western Mass. Map Pack;
$2.00 for the first book and $1.00 for each additional book.

Postage/Handling _____

Total Enclosed _____

Order Form

To order, call or write:
New England Cartographics
P.O. Box 9369, North Amherst MA 01059
(413) - 549-4124
FAX orders: (413) - 549-3621
Toll-Free (888) 995-6277

Circle one: *Mastercard*   *Visa*   *Amex*   *Check*

Card Number_____

Expiration Date _____

Signature_____

Telephone (optional) _____

Please send my order to:

Name _____

Address _____

_____

Town/City _____

State _____ **Zip** _____